THE HERITAGE OF INDIA SERIES (6)

# HYMNS OF THE TAMIL SAIVITE SAINTS

THE HERITAGE OF INDIA SERIES (6)

# HYMNS OF THE TAMIL SAIVITE SAINTS

BY

F. KINGSBURY, B. A. (Madras)

AND

G. E. PHILLIPS, B. A. (Lond.), M. A. (Oxon.)

GYAN

*Published by*

Gyan Publishing House
5, Ansari Road
Daryaganj, New Delhi-110002
Phone: 011-47034999, 9811692060
E-mail: books@gyanbooks.com

*Distribution Network*
gyanbooks.com
India, USA, Canada, UK, Australia, France



ISBN: 978-81-212-8272-7 (PB)
First Published, 1921

2nd Impression 2023

*Printed at:* Gyan Press, Delhi.



**THE HERITAGE OF INDIA SERIES (6); HYMNS OF THE TAMIL SAIVITE SAINTS**
Authors: F. KINGSBURY, G. E. PHILLIPS

*(By permission of the Director, Colombo Museum)*

ŚIVA NAṬARĀJA

THE HERITAGE OF INDIA SERIES

# HYMNS OF THE TAMIL ŚAIVITE SAINTS

BY

F. KINGSBURY, B.A. (Madras)
*(United Theological College, Bangalore)*

AND

G. E. PHILLIPS, B.A. (Lond.), M.A. (Oxon.)
*(United Theological College, Bangalore)*

ASSOCIATION PRESS
5, RUSSELL STREET, CALCUTTA

LONDON: OXFORD UNIVERSITY PRESS
NEW YORK, TORONTO, MELBOURNE,
BOMBAY, CALCUTTA AND MADRAS
1921

## AUTHORS' NOTE

This book has gone through the Press under unusually difficult circumstances. During most of the time one of the authors has been in Mesopotamia, the other in India. Partly from this cause, and partly through practical difficulties of printing, there are a few minor inconsistencies in the application of the system of transliteration.

The authors would have wished, had it been possible, to alter the note on stanza 17 (p. 27), which is there treated as a case of intercession for others. Fuller comparison of this hymn with other similar ones in Tamil religious poetry convinces them that the "she" in the hymn is none other than the devotee, who compares himself to a love-sick women, as in stanza 19.

They would also like to acknowledge their indebtedness to Dr. Farquhar, General Editor of the Series, for much hard work done in the interests of this book; also to Mrs. Phillips, Mr. G. S. Duraiswamy, B.A., and the Rev. F. Goodwill, for valuable help given with proof-reading.

The Wesleyan Mission Press, Mysore, which does not usually print Tamil, has been good enough for the sake of this book to undertake an unfamiliar task, which it has carried through with unwearied patience.

# CONTENTS



# ILLUSTRATIONS



*NOTE.—The bronze statuettes of the poets reproduced in this volume are not historical portraits but imaginative figures, created in accordance with popular traditions and used in the worship of the temple and the home.*

# INTRODUCTION

## (A)—The Hymns and their Significance

THE voice of chanting and song, to the accompaniment of unfamiliar instruments, floats out over the high wall of the temple in the coolness of the evening or the dawn, making the Western passer-by wonder what it is that is being chanted and sung. If only he had a Hindu hymn-book he thinks he could learn from it the spirit of Hinduism as well as a non-Christian could learn Christianity from Christian hymns. For the Tamil country at any rate there *is* such a hymn-book, and our present aim is to give enough specimens from it for readers to know what the hymns are like. Englishmen are wanting to understand India more than they ever wanted before, for their debt to India is heavy. Indians are wanting more than ever before to know the wonderful past of their own country, and the wonder of it is all bound up with its religion. At such a time these hymns are worth looking into, for they are being sung in temples and homes throughout the Tamil country, and Tamil is the mother-tongue of more than eighteen millions of people. For pious Śaivites they equal in authority the Sanskrit Vedas; the mere learning of them by rote is held to be a virtue, and devout Tamil parents compel their children to memorize them in much the same way as Christian parents make their children learn the Psalms.

The hymns here given are specimens from the Dēvāram and the Tiruvāchakam. The Dēvāram is the first of the collections of works held as canonical by Tamil Śaivites. Its hymns were composed between six and eight hundred A.D. by the three authors of whom this book gives some account, and the whole was put together in one collection of 797 stanzas by Nambi Āṇḍār Nambi about 1000 A.D. The Tiruvāchakam, or Sacred Utterance, was written by one author, Māṇikya Vāchaka (Tamilized as Māṇikka Vāsahar) at a date so far unsettled that scholars are still divided on the question whether it preceded or followed the Dēvāram, though most scholars place it in the ninth, or early in the tenth, century. Whenever it was written, it stands even higher than the Dēvāram in the affections of Tamil people.

Out of an immense number of hymns we have tried to select those which are most representative, those which are favourites, and those which contain the most striking thoughts. But it is amazingly difficult to give a fair or adequate idea of them in an English rendering. They are essentially songs, intended to be sung to Indian tunes, in metres which no English metre can represent. Much of their charm depends upon assonance, upon plays upon words, upon close knitting of word with word, upon intricacy of metre and rhyme, almost as much as upon the substance. We can only claim a fair degree of accuracy in our renderings, apologizing to the lovers of Tamil poetry for the plainness and poverty of our representation of so rich and varied an original. All our translations are new, and nearly all of those from the Dēvāram represent verses which have never before been done into English. One of the translators of this book learned as a Śaivite child to love these hymns, and therefore is the authority in matters of interpretation, the Englishman being responsible for the form. We shall be quite satisfied if our translations serve to call attention to the poems, and are some day replaced by worthier renderings.

We have tried to reduce introductory matter to a minimum, only giving such information as is necessary to enable readers to understand the hymns and the allusions in them. But it is entirely necessary to say something about the worship of Śiva, and to give a few words of biography of each of the four authors from whose work this book contains extracts.

## (B)—The Worship of Śiva

1. *Its history previous to these poems.*

The word Śiva occurs even in the Ṛig Veda, but there it is only in conjunction with Rudra. The joining together of these names provokes conjectures as to whether we have here an amalgamation of two earlier deities, an Aryan and a Dravidian, but these need not detain us here, since clearly even at this early date Śiva was an Aryan deity, identical with Rudra the storm-god, and father of the Maruts, storm-gods themselves. Rudra is a handsome god; he uses his thunderbolts chiefly for punishing evil-doers, and is on the whole a kindly being. The name Śiva means 'auspicious,' and must not be confused with the Tamil word for 'red,' although as it happens Rudra-Śiva was a red being.

In the period of the Purāṇas, we find that Śiva, instead of being one of a multitude of nature-deities, has risen to be one of the great triad, Brahmā, Vishṇu, and Śiva, who are far above all gods. How the change has come about we have not yet the means of discovering. The function has changed as much as the person, Śiva being now the destroyer as Brahmā is the creator and Vishṇu the preserver. The process of reduction in the number of the superior deities goes further, and Brahmā falls practically into the background, leaving only Vishṇu and Śiva as supreme beings for the worship of the people of India. By the time Hinduism penetrated southwards into the Tamil country, probably somewhere about 500 B.C., it had two main forms, the worship of Vishṇu and the worship of Śiva, the two being not too sharply disconnected. The Tamil Hindu believed in the existence of both, but held his own god, whether Śiva or Vishṇu, to be supreme. Hinduism seemed to be firmly established, but was dangerously shaken when the Jains and Buddhists spread over South India. Then came for the Vaishṇavites the teachers known as the Āḻvārs, while Śaivism was defended by the poets of whose work this book gives specimens. Hinduism was saved, but it existed henceforth in two distinct forms, Vaishṇavism and Śaivism, separated by a wider gulf than in earlier days.

2. *The portrait of Śiva and its interpretation.*

Śiva as imagined by his worshippers has a human form, usually with one but occasionally with five or six heads. He has three eyes, the right one being really the sun, the left eye the moon, and the one in the middle of his forehead fire. His reddish hair is matted in the ascetic way, and on it is the crescent moon, the Ganges, and one or more cobras, while wreathed about it is a garland of konḍai (Cassia) flowers. He has four arms, though occasional representations show eight, but one body and two legs. Commonly he is seated on a grey-coloured bull. In colour he is reddish, but his body is smeared over with white sacred ash. He holds in his hands various things such as a battle-axe, a deer, fire, a trident, a bow. Round his neck, which is dark, hangs a long necklace, the beads of which are skulls. At his waist he wears sometimes an elephant's hide, sometimes a tiger-skin, sometimes only a very scanty loin-cloth. Generally his consort, Umā, is at his left side, but sometimes he is pictured as half man and half woman, the right half (Śiva) being pink-coloured, and the left half (Umā) green or black. Śiva's abode is said to be on Mount Kailāsa in the Himālayas, but among his special haunts is the burning-ground, where bodies are cremated. One of the favourite manifestations of Śiva is that as Naṭarāja, the dancer in the great hall at Chidambaram, of which we give a picture (see frontispiece). Here Śiva has one face, four arms, and two legs, performing a spirited dance. His right foot rests on a demon named Muyalahan. He is sometimes represented as dancing along with Kāḷī, not the Kāḷī who in North India is identified with Umā, but a she-devil feared in the South.

Doubtless each of these features in the manifestation of Śiva has its history, but that is unknown at present. The legends give fanciful explanations of most of them. The tiger's skin and the elephant's hide, for instance, are those which Śiva stripped from the wild animals sent against him by the magic of his enemies the ṛishis of Darukāvana. But it is of more interest to find the religious ideas which these things suggest to a thoughtful Śaivite devotee to-day. The hides remind him that Śiva has all power, and all opposition to him is vain. That right foot of Naṭarāja set on Muyalahan means that God crushes down all evil. Those skulls in his necklace are the skulls of successive Brahmās, each of whom died after a life lasting many ages. This is a way of saying that while other gods at last come to their end, Śiva is eternal and unchanging. Śiva's dance suggests how easily, and how rhythmically, he performs his five functions of making, preserving, destroying, judging and purifying. And his dance in the burning-ground may sometimes carry the message that God becomes most real to men in the solemn hour when they part from their dead.

3. *Four common legends and their meaning.*

Of the many legends concerning Śiva four are so frequently alluded to in our poems that they should be told here, to avoid repeated explanatory notes.

1. Brahmā and Vishṇu once saw a pillar of fire that seemed to grow from the depths of the earth and to pierce beyond the highest heavens. They longed to learn its depth and height, and agreed that Brahmā should become a swan to fly to the pillar's top, and Vishṇu a boar to dig to its root. The swan flew up to the sky, but never reached the pillar's summit. The boar dug through the earth with his tusk, but never found where the pillar began. Brahmā and Vishṇu perforce acknowledged their limitations and prayed to the pillar, whereupon Śiva revealed himself, for the pillar was a form he had assumed. Not even the greatest and

wisest of creatures can by their searching find out God. But to the humble-hearted He reveals Himself.

2. Rāvaṇa, the ten-headed giant king of Ceylon, while on his conquering progress through many realms, came to the North of India and saw Kailāsa the silver mountain. Coveting its beauty he determined to uproot and transplant it to his own island. With his ten heads and twenty arms he tried to lift it from the earth, and Kailāsa shook. All the hosts of heaven, and even Umā, were terrified by what seemed to them an awful earthquake. But Śiva simply set his big toe upon the mountain, and lo, Rāvaṇa found himself being crushed to death. Repenting of his folly, Rāvaṇa prayed for mercy, and Śiva not only forgave him but even gave him fresh boons. For God pardons sinners who repent, and gives them blessings which before they did not know.

3. Three Asuras, or supernatural beings, once by doing penance obtained from Śiva three castles, one of gold, one of silver, and one of iron. These castles could fly at the owners' desire, and settle down on towns and villages, destroying many lives. In course of time the Asuras became very proud and ignored Śiva. Determining to punish them, Śiva mounted a chariot whose wheels were the sun and moon and whose seat was the earth. Brahmā was his charioteer, the four Vedas the horses, Mount Meru his bow, the ancient serpent Ādiśesha his bow-string, and Vishṇu his arrow. At sight of these preparations the gods became conceited, thinking that Śiva could not destroy his enemies without them. Śiva knowing their thoughts simply laughed, and at that laugh the three castles were on the instant reduced to ashes.

Those who forget God in their pride must be punished. When those whom God uses as his instruments begin to think themselves indispensable to him, he shews that his purposes can be fulfilled without them.

4. The gods once began to churn the ocean in the hope of obtaining divine nectar. The mountain Mandāra was their churning-stick, the primeval tortoise the pivot on which the stick rested and turned, and the serpent Vāsuki was the churning-rope. As they churned, at first great and splendid things came up. But suddenly something black rose up and darkened the whole universe. It was a mass of poison, deadly alike to gods and men. In terror of destruction, the gods and demons called on Śiva. He came, drank the poison, and saved them all. That which was enough to destroy the universe could only stain his throat with a bluish colour. That is why Śiva is often called the "poison-necked" or "blue-throated" god. There is a link here, small but real, with the Christian teaching of God as ready to suffer for the sake of humbler beings.

*(By permission of the Director, Colombo Museum)*

SAMBANDAR

# SAMBANDAR

AND HIS

# HYMNS

# I

## SAMBANDAR

### (Tamil: TIRU JÑĀNA SAMBANDAMŪRTI SWĀMĪ)

IN the first half of the seventh century A.D. the worship of Śiva was at its lowest ebb, overpowered by the Jainism and Buddhism which prevailed throughout the Tamil country. But a few pious Śaivites remained faithful. One of them, whose name means that his heart was laid at Śiva's foot, and who lived in the town in the Tanjore District now known as Shiyāli, prayed to the Śiva worshipped in the Shiyāli temple that he might be given a son who would dispel the godless dark and win men to Lord Śiva again. Sambandar's birth was the answer to that prayer. At the tender age of three, so orthodox Śaivites believe, this child was fed by Śiva's spouse with milk from her divine breast, mingled with divine wisdom, whence he is called in his full name, "The man connected with wisdom divine," Tiru Jñāna Sambandar.

He grew up to be a pilgrim poet, who visited most of the Śaivite shrines with which South India abounds, in each place singing the praise of the Śiva whom there he worshipped. The cause he loved suffered a severe blow when the great king of Madura, with many of his subjects, went over to the Jain religion. The queen-consort and her prime minister (see stanzas 20 and 21) remained faithful to Śaivism, and sent for Sambandar.

The lonely saint faced a vast multitude of Jains in the royal presence, conquered them in argument, and reconverted the king. Eight thousand of the stubborn Jains, with Sambandar's consent, were impaled alive. Later on, after a similar adventure in another of the three great kingdoms of the Tamil country of his time, Sambandar converted to Śaivism a crowd of Buddhist opponents.

This is about all that is known of a man who helped to sing Buddhism right out of Southern India, and who composed the collection of hymns which stands first among the canonical works of Śaivites. Legends make him a wonder-worker, but we must draw our knowledge of the man from his poems themselves. He certainly was skilful in the handling of the many metres in which Tamil poetry is written, and it is not impossible that his productions were as effortless as the stories of him tell. That is their weakness, for there is not very much of heart religion in them. But they seem to have powerfully helped in that process of eliminating Jainism and Buddhism from India of which we know so little, though it was complete enough to be one of the marvels of history. Their author holds the foremost place among the four great 'Śaivite Preceptors' (Śivāchāryar), and some call him the incarnation of one of the sons of Śiva.

His date seems to be one of the few clearly established dates in the history of the religion of the country. Stanza 19 shews that he was a contemporary of another great early Śaivite, whose name means "Little Servant of God," and who is known to have fought in a battle which took place in 642 A.D.

1. தோடுடையசெவியன்விடையேறியோர்தூவெண்
 மதிசூடிக்
 காடுடையசுடலைப்பொடிபூசியென்னுள்ளங்கவர்
 கள்வ
 னேடுடையமலரான்முனநாள்பணிந்தேத்தவருள்
 செய்த
 பீடுடையபிரமாபுரமேவியபெம்மானிவனன்றே.

2. உண்ணாமுலையுமையாளொடுமுடனாகியவொருவன்
 பெண்ணாகியபெருமான்மலைதிருமாமணிதிகழ
 மண்ணார்ந்தனவருவித்திரண்மழலைம்முழவதிரு
 மண்ணாமலைதொழுவார்வினைவழுவாவண்ண
 மறுமே.

We begin with the first verse which the author composed. According to the legends he uttered it at the age of three, on the banks of the temple tank at Shiyāli (once Bramāpuram), after Śiva's consort had fed him with milk from her own breast. The stanza itself of course contains no allusion to the story, but it is one of the best known verses in the Śaivite hymn-book.

1. His ears are beringed, He rideth the bull;
   His head is adorned with the crescent moon's ray;
 White is He with ash from the burning-ground swept;
   And He is the thief who my heart steals away.
 Great Brahmā enthroned on the lotus' full bloom
   Erstwhile bowed him down and His glory extolled,
 And singing received he the grace of our lord
   Who dwelleth in famèd Bramāpuram old.

---

No pilgrimage in South India is more popular than that to Tiruvaṇṇāmalai in North Arcot, the temple by a hill celebrated in many poems. Śaivism has tried to express the existence of the 'eternal feminine' in deity by giving Śiva a lady who not only is His consort, but is actually a part of Him, and is so represented in many images, which show Śiva as masculine on one side and feminine on the other.

2. He is our only Lord, conjoinèd still
   To her whose breast no sucking lips have known.
 They who in Aṇṇāmalai's holy hill,
   Where falling waters noisy chatter down,
 And the hill glistens gem-like, bow before
   Our great one who is lord and lady too,
 Unfailingly for them shall be no more
   Dread fruit of good and bad deeds they may do.

3. பறையும்பழிபாவம்படுதுயரம்பலதீரும்
பிறையும்புனலரவும்படுசடையெம்பெருமானூ
ரறையும்புனல்வருகாவிரியலைசேர்வடகரைமேல்
நிறையும்புனைமடவார்பயில்நெய்த்தானமெனீரே.

One of the first puzzles to a student of Śaivism is the way in which each of the numerous shrines seems to be spoken of as if it were Śiva's exclusive abode. The broad river marked on English maps as the Cauvery, but in Tamil called the Kāviri, which brings so much blessing to a large part of South India that the respect in which it is held is not difficult to understand, is fringed throughout its length with shrines which are believed to confer the blessings of Śiva on all who visit them. One of these is 'Neyttānam,' 'Place of Ghee.'

3. So ye but say Neyttānam is the home
Of our great Lord who wears in His long hair
The crescent moon, the river, and the snake,
Neyttānam where chaste maidens gather fair,
On the north bank of Kāviri's loud stream,
Your vileness, guiltiness, the sin you dread,
Your sorrows many, shall be banishèd.

---

This specimen of a hymn connected with Palny in the Madura District alludes (in stanza 5) to the well-known legend which says in the Śaivite way that those who love God need not fear death. Mārkandeya was a boy devoted to Śiva, but over his life hung a terrible cloud, for the fates had decreed that he would not live beyond his sixteenth year. As the appointed time drew near his father lived in an agony of dread, but Mārkandeya, free from fear, spent all his time in the worship of Śiva. The god of Death came at last. Regardless of the fact that the boy was at worship he threw over him that noose which pulls out human life from the body. The boy clung to Śiva's lingam with both his hands. From within the lingam Śiva burst forth, kicked the terrible death-god and pierced him with his trident. So Mārkandeya was saved. The scene is sculptured on many temples.

4. வேதமோதிவெண்ணூல்பூண்டுவெள்ளையெரு
தேறிப்
பூதஞ்சூழப்பொலியவருவார்புலியினுரிதோலார்
நாதாவெனவுநக்காவெனவுநம்பாவெனநின்று
பாதந்தொழுவார்பாவந்தீர்ப்பார்பழனநகராரே.

5. கண்மேற்கண்ணுஞ்சடைமேற்பிறையுமுடையா
ர்காலனைப்
புண்ணாறுதிரமெதிராறோடப்பொன்றப்புறந்
தாளா
லெண்ணாதுதைத்தவெந்தைபெருமானிமவான்
மகளோடும்
பண்ணார்களிவண்டறைபூஞ்சோலைப்பழனநக
ராரே.

6. கற்றாங்கெரியோம்பிக்கலியைவாராமே
செற்றார்வாழ்தில்லைச்சிற்றம்பலமேய
முற்றாவெண்டிங்கண்முதல்வன்பாதமே
பற்றாநின்றாரைப்பற்றாபர்வமே.

4. Holy Vedas chanting,
   Sacred thread He wears ;
All His hosts surround Him
   Whom the white bull bears.
Cometh He in splendour,
   Tiger-skin attired.
'Lord, our naked beggar
   Above all desired,'
Cry ye in your worship,
   At His feet appeal.
He who dwells in Palny
   All your sin will heal.

5. Three eyes hath His forehead,
   Fair moon crowns His hair ;
When Death sought a victim,
   Śiva's foot crashed there ;
Gory streams of blood flowed,
   Death it was that died,
Such is He, our Father,
   Umā at His side ;
Dwells He aye in Palny,
   Where bees hum around
Drunk with honeyed sweetness,
   Till its groves resound.

---

A multitude of hymns chant the glory of Chidambaram, ancient Tillai, holiest of all the Śaivite shrines. Pious Śaivites have for it a feeling not unlike the Jews' feeling for Jerusalem. The tending of the sacrificial fire comes down from pre-historic times, being firmly established when the earliest hymns of the Ṛig Veda were composed.

6. Tending as taught of old the sacrificial fire,
At Tillai Brahmans pure drive out misfortune dire.
There dwells the First of all, moon-crowned, and
      those who cleave
For ever to His foot, no cleaving sin will grieve.

2

7. மறையானை மாசிலாப்புன்சடை மல்குவெண்
பிறையானைப் பெண்ணொடாணாகியபெம்மானை
யிறையானை யேர்கொள்கச்சித்திருவேகம்பத்
துறைவானையல்லதுள்காதெனதுள்ளமே.

8. நன்றுடையானைத்தீயதில்லானைநரைவெள்ளே
றொன்றுடையானையுமையொருபாகமுடையானைச்
சென்றடையாததிருவுடையானைச்சிராப்பள்ளிக்
குன்றுடையானைக்கூறவென்னுள்ளங்குளிருமே.

9. குற்றநீகுணங்கணீகூடலாலவாயிலாய்
சுற்றநீபிரானுநீதொடர்ந்திலங்குசோதிநீ
கற்றநூற்கருத்துநீயருத்தமின்பமென்றிவை
முற்றுநீபுகழ்ந்துமுன்னுரைப்பதென்முகம்மனே.

Conjeeveram, the ancient Tamil name of which is given in this stanza, though more famous as a Vaishṇavite than as a Śaivite shrine, offers in its temples a remarkable compendium of the religious history of South India. See the article 'Kānchipuram' in Dr. Hastings' 'Encyclopædia of Religion and Ethics.'

7. He is the pith of holy writ;
 And in the tangle of His hair
The spotless crescent's ray is lit;
 He is both Lord and Lady fair.
He our great sovereign doth abide
 In Kachchi Ehambam's fair town.
My mind can think of naught beside,
 Naught beside Him, and Him alone.

---

The next two stanzas, taken from two separate hymns associated with the great cities of Trichinopoly and Madura, both sacred places of Śaivism, are set side by side in order to bring out a point which even the most sympathetic student may not ignore. Śiva is commonly spoken of as all good, as in stanza 8, and yet not infrequently He includes, as in stanza 9, both good and its opposite. The pantheistic tendency even in these hymns causes God to be sometimes depicted as so all-embracing as to include evil as well as good.

8. All goodness hath He and no shadow of ill.
 Grey-white is His bull, fair Umā shares His form.
His wealth is past searching. Chirāpaḷḷi's hill
 Is His, whom to praise keeps my heart ever warm.

9. Thou art right and Thou art wrong,
 Lord of holy Ālavāy;
Kinsman, I to Thee belong;
 Never fades Thy light away.
Thou the sense of books divine,
 Thou my wealth, my bliss art Thou,
Thou my all, and in Thy shrine
 With what praises can I bow?

10. ஆதியாயநான்முகனுமாலுமறிவரிய
சோதியானே நீதியில்லேன் சொல்லுவதுன்
றிறமே
ஓதிநாளுமுன்னையேத்துமென்னைவினையவலம்
வாதியாமே வந்துநல்காய் வலிவலமேயவனே.

No one can know Śiva unless He chooses to reveal Himself. This thought constantly recurs with great emphasis. Its favourite expression is in the first legend of the four told in our introduction. Hymn singers are fond of contrasting with the vain search of Brahmā and Vishṇu the revelation of Himself which Śiva has graciously granted to them. Compare stanzas 25 and 48.

10. Thou Light whom Brahmā, being's fount, and Vishṇu could not see,
No righteousness have I, I only speak in praise of Thee.
Come, Valivalam's Lord, let no dark fruit of deeds, I pray,
Torment Thy slave who with his song extols Thee day by day.

---

Astrology plays a large part in popular Hinduism, and the influence of baleful or auspicious stars must be reckoned with in daily life. Most baleful of all is the influence of the eclipse, which is caused by two dragons Rāhu and Kētu which swallow the moon or the sun. This stanza enumerates the nine planets, Sun, Moon, Mars, Mercury, Jupiter, Venus, Saturn, Rāhu and Kētu, and says that to the singer, who has Śiva in his heart, all of them, even the dragons of eclipse, are auspicious. It is a powerful and characteristically Hindu way of saying that all things work together for good to those who love God.

The reference to the bamboo constantly recurs in descriptions of ladies' beauty. Everyone who has seen a feathery clump of bamboo trees waving in the breeze will understand it as a symbol of delicate grace.

The vīṇa is the most delicate and beautiful instrument played in South India.

11. வேயுறுதோளிபங்கன் விடமுண்டகண்டன் மிக
நல்லவீணை தடவி
மாசறு திங்கள் கங்கைமுடிமேலணிந்தெ னுள
மேபுகுந்தவதனா
ஞாயிறு திங்கள் செவ்வாய்புதன் வியாழம் வெள்ளி
சனிபாம்பிரண்டுமுடனே
யாசறுநல்லநல்லவவைநல்லநல்லவடியாரவர்க்கு
மிகவே.

12. மந்திரமாவது நீறுவானவர்மேலது நீறு
சுந்தரமாவது நீறு துதிக்கப்படுவது நீறு
தந்திரமாவது நீறுசமயத்திலுள்ளது நீறு
செந்துவர்வாயுமைபங்கன் றிருவாலவாயான்
றிருநீறே.

11. She shares His form whose shoulders' curve vies with the bamboo's grace.
His throat the poison drank, He touched the vīṇa into tune.
The lustrous moon and Ganges crown His hair, and He a place
Hath made Himself within my heart. Wherefore let shine the moon
Or sun or any star of good or ill, or serpents twain.
For Śiva's slave all are benign, all work for him great gain.

---

White ash from burnt cow-dung must be worn by all true Śaivites. Every day the worshipper, facing north-east and crying 'Śiva, Śiva,' must dip in the ash the fingers of his right hand and draw the three middle fingers from left to right along his forehead, so leaving three horizontal white lines. The ceremonial side of Śaivism is so prominent that this one stanza must be given, a specimen of many extolling the virtues and potencies of the ash.

The Tantras are works inculcating ceremonies, also magic performances and mystic rites. Some of these are of an immoral nature.

12. The sacred ash has mystic power,
'Tis worn by dwellers in the sky.
The ash bestows true loveliness.
Praise of the ash ascends on high.
The ash shows what the Tantras mean,
And true religion's essence tells,
The ash of Him of Ālavāy,
In whom red-lippèd Umā dwells.

13. காதலாகிக்கசிந்துகண்ணீர்மல்கி
யோதுவார்தமைநன்னெறிக்குய்ப்பது
வேதநான்கினுமெய்ப்பொருளாவது
நாதனாம நமச்சிவாயவே.

14. சித்தந்தெளிவீர்கா, ளத்தனாரூரைப்
பத்திமலர்தூவ, முத்தியாகுமே.

15. பிறவியறுப்பீர்கா, ளறவனாரூரை
மறவாதேத்துமின், றுறவியாகுமே.

16. துன்பந்துடைப்பீர்கா, ளன்பனணியாரூர்
நன்பொன்மலர்தூவ, வின்பமாகுமே.

Equally important with the wearing of the sacred ash is the constant repetition of the five syllables, or panchākshara, 'Namaśivāya.' This, which means literally 'a bow to Śiva,' is the chief mantra or mystic utterance of Śaivism. In Śaivite catechisms a whole chapter is devoted to its uses.

13. Those who repeat it while love's tears outpour,
It gives them life, and guides them in the way.
'Tis the true substance of the Vedas four,
The Lord's great name, wherefore 'Hail Śiva,' say.

---

The next three stanzas are from a hymn written in a very attractive short-lined metre, and promise light, freedom from rebirth, and bliss, through devotion to Śiva at Ārūr (now Tiruvaḷḷūr in the Tanjore District).

14. For the Father in Ārūr
Sprinkle ye the blooms of love;
In your heart will dawn true light,
Every bondage will remove.

15. Him the holy in Ārūr
Ne'er forget to laud and praise;
Bonds of birth will severed be,
Left behind all worldly ways.

16. In Ārūr, our loved one's gem,
Scatter golden blossoms fair.
Sorrow ye shall wipe away,
Yours be bliss beyond compare.

17. சடையாயெனுமால்சரணீயெனுமால்
விடையாயெனுமால்வெருவாவிழுமால்
மடையார்குவளைம்மலரும்மருக
லுடையாய்தகுமோவிவளுண்மெலிவே.

18. புத்தரோடுபொறியில்சமணும்புறங்கூறநெறிநில்லா
வொத்தசொல்லவுலகம்பலிதேர்ந்தெனதுள்ள
ங்கவர்கள்வன்
மத்தயானைமறுகவ்வுரிபோர்த்ததோர்மாயம்மி
துவென்னப்
பித்தர்போலும்பிரமாபுரமேவியபெம்மானிவ
னன்றே.

Associated with the hymn from which our next verse is taken is a story of the author, Sambandar, helping a sorrowing woman by raising to life the man she loved, who had been killed by snake-bite. The hymn makes no allusion to such a miracle, but it does give an example of intercession on behalf of another, an element which is somewhat rare in these devotional books.

17. Prostrate with fear at Thy feet she cries 'Lord with matted hair, my Refuge, Rider of the bull!' Lord of Maruhal where fresh water-lilies bloom, is it right to leave her in this anguish of heart?

---

Our present writer's poems contain such frequent denunciations of Buddhism or Jainism that it is clear that they were written at a time when the struggle between Hinduism and these other religions was at its height. Buddhism and Jainism are scarcely known in South India to-day, though at one time they were supreme. It is probable that these songs helped not a little to drive them out of the country.

18. Those Buddhists and mad Jains may slander speak.
Such speech befits the wand'rers from the way.
But He who came to earth and begged for alms,
He is the thief who stole my heart away.
The raging elephant charged down at Him;
O marvel! He but took and wore its hide;
Madman men think Him, but He is the Lord
Who in great Bramāpuram doth abide.

19. பைங்கோட்டுமலர்ப்புன்னைப்பறவைகாள்பய
    ப்பூரச்
சங்காட்டந்தவிர்த்தென்னைத்தவிராநோய்
    தந்தானே
செங்காட்டங்குடிமேயசிறுத்தொண்டன்பணி
    செய்ய
வெங்காட்டுளனலேந்திவிளையாடும்பெருமானே.

The "Little Servant of God" mentioned in the next verse is one of the 63 canonized saints of Śaivism. According to the collection of legends known as the Periya Purāṇam, which is a Tamil Śaivite classic, he fought at the battle of Vādāpi, the modern Badāmi, which took place in 642 A.D. There are other indications which strengthen the view that these hymns date from the seventh century A.D.

In the first three lines of the verse Śiva is conceived as a lover, and the devotee as the woman whom He loves. In India the pain of absence from a lover is supposed to cause spots to appear on the skin of the woman who loves.

19. Birds in the flowering green-branched puṇṇai tree,
Love writeth clear its marks on me, for He
Who cured my grief, yet left unending pain.
Senkāṭṭankuḍi is His holy fane,
And there His "Little Servant" dwells, who now
And ever doth before Lord Śiva bow.
There in the burning-ground, with fire in hand,
Sporteth unceasingly our Master grand.

---

Another possible indication of date occurs in the next two verses, given in English prose because the Tamil names will not fit into English metres. The Mangaiyarkkarasi here mentioned was the wife of a king of Madura, Kūn Pāṇḍiyan, known to history. According to the above-mentioned collection of stories, this king became a Jain. Then the queen and the prime minister named in our poem sent for Sambandar, our author, through whose efforts the king was reconverted, and all Jain teachers were executed by impaling. Unfortunately the date of Kūn Pāṇḍiyan cannot at present be accurately determined. An able discussion of it can be seen in "The Tamilian Antiquary, No. 3."

20. மங்கையர்க்கரசிவளவர்கோன்பாவைவரிவளைக்
கைமடமானி
பங்கயச்செல்விபாண்டிமாதேவிபணிசெய்துநா
டொறும்பரவப்
பொங்கழலுருவன்பூதநாயகனால்வேதமும்பொ
ருள்களுமருளி
யங்கயற்கண்ணிதன்னொடுமமர்ந்தவாலவாயா
வதுமிதுவே.

21. வெற்றவேயடியாரடிமிசைவீழும்விருப்பினன்
வெள்ளைநீறணியுங்
கொற்றவன்றனக்குமந்திரியாயகுலச்சிறைகுலாவி
நின்றேத்து
மொற்றைவெள்விடையனும்பரார்தலைவனுலகினி
லியற்கையையொழித்திட்
டற்றவர்க்கற்றசிவனுறைகின்றவாலவாயாவது
மிதுவே.

The explanation of the term 'Fish-eyed maid,' which sounds curiously in English ears, is that in Madura Siva's consort is called Mīnākshi, *i.e.* fish-eyed. The suggestion of the epithet, frequently applied to beautiful women, is that the motion of their eyes resembles the beautiful motion of a fish in water.

20. This is Ālavāy, where dwells the flame-formed lord of hosts, giver of the four Vedas and their meaning, with the fair fish-eyed maid. Here, reigning like the goddess of good fortune, Mangaiyarkkarasi the Chōḻa king's daughter, braceletted chaste Pāṇdiyan queen, daily serves and praises God.

---

The poem from which 20 and 21 are taken consists of stanzas like these alternately praising the queen and the king's minister, the last verse praising them both together.

21. This is Ālavāy, Śiva's abode. To those who forsake the world He reveals Himself as world-forsaking too. Head of the heavenly ones, He rides the one white bull. Praised is He by Kulachchiṛai, minister of that monarch who wears white ash, and loves to lay himself bare at the feet of Śiva's slaves.

---

Once, says a story, when Sambandar was about to contend with the Jains, the queen feared the consequences which might befal him, but he assured her in this verse that he could dare all when his God of Madura was on his side.

22. மானினேர்விழிமாதராய்வழுதிக்குமாபெருந்
தேவிகேள்
பானல்வாயொருபாலனீங்கிவனென்றுநீபரிவெய்
திடே
லானைமாமலையாதியாயவிடங்களிற்பலவல்லல்சே
ரீனர்கட்கெளியேனலேன்றிருவாலவாயரனிற்கவே.

23. செய்யனே திருவாலவாய்மேவிய
ஐயனேயஞ்சலென்றருள்செய்யெனைப்
பொய்யராமமணர்கொளுவுஞ்சுடர்
பையவேசென் றுபாண்டியற்காகவே.

24. வாழ்க வந்தணர் வானவ ரானினம்
வீழ்க தண்புனல் வேந்தனு மோங்குக
ஆழ்க தீயதெல் லாமர னாமமே
சூழ்க வையக முந்துயர் தீர்கவே.

22. O fair one with the deer's glance meek,
Pāṇḍya's great queen, think not of me
As of some sucking infant weak,
Because such wicked foes there be.
If only Hara by me stand,
Stronger am I than all their band.

---

The story here is that the Jains had set fire to Sambandar's house. He prayed in this stanza that the fire, transformed into a fever, might go to the Pāṇḍyan king, then a Jain. It did so, and the king was converted.

23. O Thou whose form is fiery red,
In holy Ālavāy, our Sire,
In grace deliver me from dread.
False Jains have lit for me a fire:
O, let it to the Pāṇḍyan ruler go,
That he the torture of slow flame may know.

---

Our specimens of Sambandar's poetry may end with a verse which is a kind of benediction, often set as an auspicious word on the front page of a book.

24. Blest be the Brāhmans pure, the heavenly ones, and kine.
Cool rain fall on the earth! May the king's glory shine!
Perish all forms of ill! Let Hara's name resound!
May sorrow pass away, from earth's remotest bound.

*(By permission of the Director, Colombo Museum)*

APPARSWĀMĪ

# APPARSWAMI
AND HIS
# HYMNS

## II.

# TIRUNĀVUKKARASU SWĀMI

(More commonly referred to as APPARSWĀMI)

SAMBANDAR, whose works we have been studying, had a friend older than himself, named Appar, or Tirunāvukkarasu, belonging to that Veḷḷāḷa caste which to this day makes a very solid element in the population of the Tamil country. Left an orphan at an early age, Appar was brought up by a loving elder sister as a pious devotee of Śiva. Great was the sister's grief when Appar forsook the faith of his fathers and became a religious teacher among the Jains. But her earnest prayers at last prevailed, and Appar not only came back to Śaivism himself, but was the means of reconverting to Śaivism the king of his country. His full name was Tirunāvukkarasu, or 'King of the Tongue', but his young friend Sambandar called him Appar, or Father, and the name stuck to him. He too wandered throughout the Tamil country, sometimes alone, sometimes in company with Sambandar, singing his way from shrine to shrine. Pictures show him holding in his hand a little tool for scraping grass, with which he used to scrape the stones of the temple courts. The Jains persecuted him, and many stories tell of his miraculous escapes from their hands.

His hymns show a truly religious nature, with a deep-rooted sense of sin and need, and an exalted joy in God. There is real critical acumen in the old epigram which represents Śiva as appraising the three great writers of the Dēvāram, or Śaivite hymn-book:— "Sambandar praised himself; Sundarar praised Me for pelf; My Appar praised Me Myself."

25. திருவினாள்கொழுநனாருந்திசைமுகமுடையக
கோவும்
இருவருமெழுந்தும்வீழ்ந்துமிணையடிகாணமா
ட்டார்
ஒருவனேயெம்பிரானேயுன்றிருப்பாதங்காண்பான்
அருவனேயருளவேண்டுமதிகைவீரட்டனாரே.

26. கடவுந்திகிரிகடவாதொழியக்கயிலையுற்றான்
படவுந்திருவிரரொன்றுவைத்தாய்பனிமால்
வரைபோல்
இடபம்பொறித்தென்னையேன்றுகொள்ளா
யிருஞ்சோலைதிங்கள்
தடவுங்கடந்தையுட்டூங்கானைமாடத்தெந்தத்
துவனே.

God, the essentially unsearchable, in His grace will reveal Himself to men. (See the first of the legends told in the Introduction.) Athihai Vīraṭṭānam, in the South Arcot District, is the shrine here commemorated.

25. Vishṇu, spouse of Lakshmi, and four-ways-facing Brahm,
Searched the heights and depths, but Thy feet could never see.
Yet, O only Lord, who in Athihai dost dwell,
Formless, in Thy grace, grant the sight of them to me.

---

The notable thing about our next verse is not so much the legend of the crushing of Rāvaṇa, who tried to storm the mountain Kailāsa, where Śiva had His heaven, but rather the thought of the devotee being stamped as the property of his god, a thought which recurs in other hymns. According to tradition Apparswāmi did receive the Hindu equivalent of St. Francis' stigmata, the mark of Śiva's bull as if branded on his body. We cannot help recalling St. Paul's expression in Galatians vi. 17.

26. All other worlds his sceptre swayed,
But when Kailāsa he would rule
Thy crushing foot presumption paid.
O stamp me with Thy sacred bull,
White as Himāl'ya's snowy hill.
Accept me, O our truth divine,
There where the moon outsoareth still
Groves of Tūṅgānaimāḍam's shrine.

27. வடிவேறு திரிசூலந் தோன்றுந்தோன்றும்
வளர்சடைமேலிளமதியந் தோன்றுந்தோன்றுங்
கடியேறுகமழ் கொன்றைக்கண்ணி தோன்றுங்
காதில்வெண்குழைதோடுகலந்துதோன்றும்
இடியேறுகளிற்றுரிவைப் போர்வைதோன்றும்
எழிறிகழுந்திருமுடியுமிலங்கித்தோன்றும்
பொடியேறுதிருமேனி பொலிந்துதோன்றும்
பொழிறிகழும் பூவணத்தெம் புனிதனார்க்கே.

28. ஒருவனாயுலகேத்த நின்றநாளோ
வோருருவேமூவுருவமானநாளோ
கருவனாய்க்காமனைமுன் காய்ந்தநாளோ
காமனையுங்கண்ணழலால்விழித்தநாளோ
மருவனாய் மண்ணும்விண்ணுந்தெரித்தநாளோ
மான்மறிக்கையேந்தியோர் மாதோர்பாகந்
திருவினாற் சேர்வதற்கு முன்னோபின்னோ
திருவாரூர்கோயிலாக்கொண்டநாளே.

Here is the divine vision as the enraptured Śaivite sees it.

27. See, there His bright trident appears to me ;
    See, there is the moon in His tangled hair ;
His garland of flowers from the kondai tree,
    And the ear-ring white in His either ear,
The cloak that He tore from the elephant wild,
    His glittering crown and His body's sheen.
Ash-smeared, He is ever the undefiled,
    In Pūvaṇam circled by groves all green.

---

The singer, standing at the shrine of Tiruvalur (Ārūr) in the Tanjore district, muses over the ancient connection of his lord with the holy place, suggesting that it began before the creation, before Śiva wrought his greatest marvels, perhaps even before the one Supreme, Īśvara, expanded into the triad Brahmā, Vishṇu and Rudra.

28. When was that ancient day our Lord
    Chose Ārūr should His temple be ?
Was't when He stood 'mid praising worlds
    Alone, or when the One grew three ?
Was't when in wrath He burned up Death,
    Or turned on Lust His flaming eye ?
Or when creative, immanent,
    He called to being earth and sky ?
Was't when, his young deer in his hand,
    He came, with Umā as His part ?
Or ere He joined that lady fair
    Took He our Ārūr to His heart ?

29. நீதியால்வாழமாட்டேனித்தலுந்தூயேனல்லேன்
ஓதியுமுணரமாட்டேனுன்னையுள்வைக்கமாட்டேன்
சோதியேசுடரேயுன்றன்றாமலர்ப்பாதங்காண்பான்
ஆதியேயலைந்துபோனேனதிகைவீரட்டனாரே.

30. தெருளுமாதெருளமாட்டேன்றீவினைச்சுற்ற
மென்னும்
பொருளுளேயழுந்திநாளும்போவதோர்நெறி
யுங்காணேன்
இருளுமாமணிகண்டாநின்னிணையடியிரண்டுங்
காண்பான்
அருளுமாறருளவேண்டுமதிகைவீரட்டனாரே.

31. உறுகயிறூசல்போலவொன்றுவிட்டொன்றுபற்றி
மறுகயிறூசல்போலவந்துவந்துலவுநெஞ்சம்
பெறுகயிறூசல்போலப்பிறைபுல்குசடையாய்
பாதத்
தறுகயிறூசலானேனதிகைவீரட்டனாரே.

It is often said, not without truth, that Hinduism fails to create a strong sense of sin. But there are great exceptions: witness the following verses, samples of many, taken from a hymn which trembles with feeling. The author is sunk in sin. Or he has been like a swing, flying first toward evil and then towards God; but now, joy! the cord has snapped, and he lies fixed at his Lord's feet. Yet the old mood returns; his soul is bound and drugged with sleep, and life has no joys to offer unless God will save.

### The Soul's Bitter Cry

29. In right I have no power to live,
    Day after day I'm stained with sin;
I read, but do not understand;
    I hold Thee not my heart within.
O light, O flame, O first of all,
    I wandered far that I might see,
Athihai Vīraṭṭānam's Lord,
    Thy flower-like feet of purity.

30. Daily I'm sunk in worldly sin;
    Naught know I as I ought to know;
Absorbed in vice as 'twere my kin,
    I see no path in which to go.
O Thou with throat one darkling gem,
    Gracious, such grace to me accord,
That I may see Thy beauteous feet,
    Athihai Vīraṭṭānam's Lord.

31. My fickle heart one love forsakes,
    And forthwith to some other clings;
Swiftly to some one thing it sways,
    And e'en as swiftly backward swings.
O Thou with crescent in Thy hair,
    Athihai Vīraṭṭānam's Lord,
Fixed at Thy feet henceforth I lie,
    For Thou hast broken my soul's cord.

32. கழித்திலேன்காமவெங்நோய்காதன்மையென்
னும்பாசம்
ஒழித்திலேனூன்கணோக்கியுணர்வெனுமிமைதிற
ந்து
விழித்திலேன்வெளிறுதோன்றவினையெனுஞ்சர
க்குக்கொண்டேன்
அழித்திலேனயர்த்துப்போனேனதிகைவீர
ட்டனாரே.

33. ஓம்பினேன்கூட்டைவாளாவுள்ளத்தோர்கொடு
மைவைத்துக்
காம்பிலாமூழைபோலக்கருதிற்றேமுகக்கமா
ட்டேன்
பாம்பின்வாய்த்தேரைபோலப்பலபலநினைக்கின்
றேனை
யோம்பிநீயுய்யக்கொள்ளாயொற்றியூருடைய
கோவே.

34. மனமெனுந்தோணிபற்றிமதியெனுங்கோலையூன்றிச்
சினமெனுஞ்சரக்கையேற்றிச்செறிகடலோடும்
போது
மதனெனும்பாறைதாக்கிமறியும்போதறிய
வொண்ணா
துனையுமுணர்வைநல்காயொற்றியூருடைய
கோவே.

32. The bond of lust I cannot break ;
 Desire's fierce torture will not die ;
My soul I cannot stab awake
 To scan my flesh with seeing eye.
I bear upon me load of deeds,
 Load such as I can ne'er lay down.
Athihai Vīraṭṭānam's Lord,
 Weary of joyless life I've grown.

---

Fresh pictures in another hymn set forth his sad condition. God's vessels are full of the sweetness of grace, but his spoon has no handle. He feels himself in the deadly grasp of fate, like the frog in the cruel mouth of the snake which is slowly swallowing it down. Or he is on a raft on the sea of life, wrecked on the rock of lust.

33. While violence is in my heart,
 Care of my body cage is vain.
My spoon no handle hath when I
 Thy honey's grace to drink am fain.
As in the serpent's mouth the frog,
 Caught in life's terrors, wild I rave.
Thou, King of holy Ottiyūr,
 Wilt Thou not care for me and save ?

34. When on life's angry waves I launch,
 My heart's the raft I take to me,
My mind's the pole I lean upon,
 Vexation's freight I bear to sea.
I strike upon the rock of lust !
 O then, though witless quite I be,
Grant, King of holy Ottiyūr,
 Such wisdom that I think of Thee.

35. குலம்பொல்லேன் குணம்பொல்லேன் குறியும்பொ
ல்லேன்
குற்றமேபெரிதுடையேன்கோலமாய
நலம்பொல்லேனான்பொல்லேன் ஞானியல்லே
னல்லாரோடிசைந்திலேனடுவேனின்ற
விலங்கலேன்விலங்கலாதொழிந்தேனல்லேன்
வெறுப்பனவுமிகப் பெரிதும்பேசவல்லேன்
இலம்பொல்லேனிரப்பதல்லால் ஈயமாட்டே
னென்செய்வான்றோன்றினே னேழையேனே

36. நில்லாதநீர்சடைமேனிற்பித்தானை
நினையாவென்னெஞ்சைநினைவித்தானைக்
கல்லாதனவெல்லாங்கற்பித்தானைக்
காணாதனவெல்லாங் காட்டினானைச்
சொல்லாதனவெல்லாஞ் சொல்லியென்னைத்
தொடர்ந்திங் கடியேனையாளாக்கொண்டு
பொல்லாவென்னோய்தீர்த்த புனிதன்றன்னைப்
புண்ணியனைப்பூந்துருத்திக்கண்டேனானே.

It would be hard to find a more comprehensive confession of sin than our next stanza from another hymn.

35. Evil, all evil, my race, evil my qualities all,
Great am I only in sin, evil is even my good.
Evil my innermost self, foolish, avoiding the pure,
Beast am I not, yet the ways of the beast I can never forsake.
I can exhort with strong words, telling men what they should hate,
Yet can I never give gifts, only to beg them I know.
Ah! wretched man that I am, whereunto came I to birth?

---

We give next a series of stanzas in various metres from different hymns, in which the saint utters in song some of the joy which his religion has brought him. God has revealed mysteries to him which tongue cannot tell, and dwells in his life's innermost places. God is to him the fabled katpaha tree, supplying his every need. God is his all in all, and His presence is sweeter than melody or evening moonlight.

36. The moving water He made stand unmoving in His hair;
And He my thoughtless heart hath fixed in thought of Him alone;
He taught me that which none can learn, what none can see laid bare;
What tongue tells not He told; me He pursued and made His own.
The spotless pure, the holy One, my fell disease He healed,
And in Pūṇturutti to me, e'en me, Himself revealed.

37. திருவேயென் செல்வமே தேனே வானோர்
செழுஞ்சுடரே செழுஞ்சுடர்நற் சோதி மிக்க
உருவேயென் னுறவே யென் னூனே யூனி
னுள்ளமே யுள்ளத்தி னுள்ளே நின்ற
கருவேயென் கற்பகமே கண்ணே கண்ணிற்
கருமணியே மணியாடு பாவாய் காவாய்
அருவாய வல்வினைநோ யடையா வண்ண
மாவடுதண் டுறையுறையு மமரரேறே

38. அப்பனீ யம்மைநீ யையனுநீ
யன்புடைய மாமனுமாமியுநீ
ஒப்புடையமாதருமொண்பொருளுநீ
யொருகுலமுஞ்சுற்றமுமோரூருநீ
துய்ப்பனவுமுய்ப்பனவுந்தோற்றுவாய்நீ
துணையாயென்னெஞ்சந்துறப்பிப்பாய்நீ
இப்பொன்னீ யிம்மணிநீ யிம்முத்துநீ
யிறைவனீயேறூர்ந்தசெல்வனீயே.

39. மாசில் வீணையு மாலை மதியமும்
வீசு தென்றலும் வீங்கிளவேனிலு
மூசு வண்டறை பொய்கையும் போன்றதே
ஈச னெந்தை யிணையடி நீழலே.

37. O wealth, my treasure, sweetness, lustre fair of heavenly hosts,
Of lustre glory that excels,-embodied One, my kin,
My flesh, yea heart within my flesh, image within my heart,
My all-bestowing tree, my eye, pupil my eye within,
Picture seen in that pupil, lord of Āḍuturai cool,
Immortals' king, keep far from me strong pain of fruits of sin.

38. Thou to me art parents, Lord,
Thou all kinsmen that I need,
Thou to me art loved ones fair,
Thou art treasure rich indeed.
Family, friends, home art Thou,
Life and joy I draw from Thee,
False world's good by Thee I leave,
Gold, pearl, wealth art Thou to me.

39. As the vīṇa's pure sound, as the moonlight at even,
As the south wind's soft breath, as the spring's growing heat,
As the pool hovered over by whispering bees,
So sweet is the shade at our Father-Lord's feet.

40. நாமார்க்குங் குடியல்லோநமனை யஞ்சோ
நரகத்திலிடர்ப்படோ நடலையில்லோ
மேமாப்போம்பிணியறியோம் பணிவோமல்லோ
மின்பமே யெந்நாளுந் துன்பமில்லை
தாமார்க்குங் குடியல்லாத் தன்மையான
சங்கரனற் சங்கவெண்குழையோர் காதிற்
கோமாற்கே நாமென்று மீளாவாளாய்க்
கொய்ம்மலர்ச்சேவடியிணையே குறுகினோமே.

41. சங்கநிதிபதுமநிதி யிரண்டுந்தந்து
தரணியொடுவானாளத்தருவரேனு
மங்குவாரவர்செல்வமதிப்போமல்லோ
மாதேவர்க்கேகாந்தரல்லராகில்
அங்கமெலாங்குறைந்தழுகுதொழுநோயரா
யாவுரித்துத்தின்றுழலும்புலையரேனுங்
கங்கைவார்சடைக்கரந்தார்க் கன்பராகி
லவர்கண்டீர்நாம்வணங்குங்கடவுளாரே.

40. No man holds sway o'er us,
Nor death nor hell fear we;
No tremblings, griefs of mind,
No pains nor cringings see.
Joy, day by day, unchanged
Is ours, for we are His,
His ever, who doth reign,
Our Śaṅkara, in bliss.
Here to His feet we've come,
Feet as plucked flow'rets fair;
See how His ears divine
Ring and white couch-shell wear.

41. Though they give me the jewels from Indra's abode,
Though they grant me dominion o'er earth, yea o'er heaven,
If they be not the friends of our lord Mahādēv,
What care I for wealth by such ruined hands giv'n?
But if they love Śiva, who hides in His hair
The river of Gaṅga, then whoe'er they be,
Foul lepers, or outcastes, yea slayers of kine,
To them is my homage, gods are they to me.

---

Often the Hindu devotee asks and re-asks the fundamental question 'Who am I?', coming to the saddest of conclusions, but setting against the background of his delusive life of self the great reality of God, to worship whom is to find release from the prison-house of personality.

42. தந்தையார்தாயாருடன் பிறந்தார்
தாரமார் புத்திரரார்தாந்தாமாரே
வந்தவாறெங்ஙனேபோமாறேதோ
மாயமாமிதற்கேது மகிழவேண்டா
சிந்தையீருமக்கொன்று சொல்லக்கேண்மின்
றிகழ்மதியும்வாளரவுந்திளைக்குஞ்சென்னி
எந்தையார்திருநாமநமச்சிவாய
வென்றெழுவார்க்கிருவிசும்பிலிருக்கலாமே.

43. தலையேநீவணங்காய்—தலை—மாலைதலைக்கணிந்து
தலையாலேபலிதேருந்தலைவனைத்·தலையேநீவணங்
காய்

44. கண்காள் காண்மின்களோ·கட·னஞ்சுண்டக
ண்டன்றன்னை
யெண்டோள் வீசிநின்றாடும் பிரான்றன்னைக்·க
ண்காள் காண்மின்களோ.

42. Thy father, mother, brethren, wife,
 Ask thyself who are they?
Thy children; yea, thy very self,
 Who art thou, canst thou say?
How cam'st thou here, how wilt depart?
 Love not this world unreal.
Ye anxious souls, this lesson learn,
 To one pure name appeal.
Our father He, crowned with the moon
 And snake. Who Him adore,
Prone lying, with "Hail Śiva, hail,"
 In heav'n live evermore.

---

Our next hymn with the short-lined verses (nos. 43 to 48) is a kind of Śaivite consecration hymn, mentioning successively various parts of the body—head, eyes, ears—to be given to the worship of Śiva. Verse 46 must sound sadly to a Śaivite, for it is frequently sung in the ears of the dying, as a plaintive appeal to think of God. Verse 47 rises far above the usual ideas of future absorption to the thought of a blissful state of communion with and praise of God.

43. Head of mine, bow to Him,
 True Head, skull garlanded,
A skull was His strange begging-bowl,
 Bow low to Him, my head.

44. Eyes of mine, gaze on Him
 Who drank the dark sea's bane.
Eight arms He brandishes in dance,
 At Him agaze remain.

45. செவிகாள் கேண்மின்களோ-சிவ-னெம்மிறை செ
ம்பவள
மெரிபோன் மேனிப்பிரான்றிறமெப்போதுஞ்-
செவிகாள்கேண்மின்களோ.

46. உற்றாருளரோ-உயிர்-கொண்டுபோம்பொழுது
குற்றாலத்துறை கூத்தனல்லானமக் குற்றாரு
ளரோ.

47. இறுமாந்திருப்பன்கொலோ ஈசன்-பல்கணத்தெ
ண்ணப்பட்டுச்
சிறுமானேந்திதன்சேவடிக் கீழ்ச்சென்றங் கிறு
மாந்திருப்பன்கொலோ

48. தேடிக்கண்டுகொண்டேன்-திரு-மாலொடுநான்
முகனுந்
தேடித்தேடொணாத்தேவனையென்னுள்ளே தே
டிக்கண்டுகொண்டேன்.

45. Ears of mine, hear His praise,
    Śiva, our flaming king.
Flaming as coral red His form:
    Ears, hear men praises sing.

46. What kinsmen in that hour
    When life departs, have we?
Who but Kuṭṭālam's dancing lord
    Can then our kinsman be?

47. How proud shall I be there,
    One of His heavenly host,
At His fair feet who holds the deer,
    How proud will be my boast!

48. I sought Him and I found.
    Brahm sought in vain on high.
Vishṇu delved vainly underground.
    Him in my soul found I.

---

The mystic can never be a satisfied ceremonialist. These Śaivite devotees commonly praise the god of a particular shrine in language which might suggest that Śiva is only to be found there. And everyone who knows India remembers the ceaseless streams of pilgrims journeying to the Ganges or the Cauvery (Tamil Kāviri), to Rāmēśwaram or Cape Comorin or a hundred other holy places. But with a fine inconsistency these ancient singers sometimes point men away from externalities to a worship inward and spiritual; witness the following hymn. As to the terms used in v. 50, Vedas are the religious works of the highest authority, Śāstras are philosophical and practical works based on them, while Vēdāngas are sciences subordinate to the Vedas, and there are six of them.

49. கங்கையாடிலென் காவிரியாடிலென்
கொங்குதண்குமரித்துறையாடிலெ
னோங்குமாகடலோ தநீராடிலெ
னெங்குமீசனெனாதவர்க்கில்லையே.

50. வேதமோதிலென் சாத்திரங்கேட்கிலெ
னீதிநூல்பலநித்தல்பயிற்றிலெ
னோதியங்கமோராறுமுணரிலெ
னீசனையுள்குவார்க்கன்றியில்லையே.

51. கானநாடுகலந்துதிரியிலெ
னீனமின்றியிருந்தவஞ்செய்யிலெ
னூனையுண்டலொழிந்துவானோக்கிலென்
ஞானனென்பவர்க்கன்றிநன்கில்லையே.

52. நன்றுநோற்கிலென் பட்டினியாகிலென்
குன்றமேறியிருந்தவஞ்செய்யிலென்
சென்றுநீரிற்குளித்துத்திரியிலெ
னென்றுமீசனென்பார்க்கன்றியில்லையே.

49. Why bathe in Gaṅga's stream, or Kāviri?
Why go to Comorin in Koṅgu's land?
Why seek the waters of the sounding sea?
Release is theirs, and theirs alone, who call
In every place upon the Lord of all.

50. Why chant the Vedas, hear the Śāstras' lore?
Why daily teach the books of righteousness?
Why the Vēdāngas six say o'er and o'er?
Release is theirs, and theirs alone, whose heart
From thinking of its Lord shall ne'er depart.

51. Why roam the jungle, wander cities through?
Why plague life with unstinting penance hard?
Why eat no flesh, and gaze into the blue?
Release is theirs, and theirs alone, who cry
Unceasing to the Lord of wisdom high.

52. Why fast and starve, why suffer pains austere?
Why climb the mountains, doing penance harsh?
Why go to bathe in waters far and near?
Release is theirs, and theirs alone, who call
At every time upon the Lord of all.

---

It looks like a sudden drop when the same writer in our next hymn seems to say that everything depends upon the pronunciation of the five sacred syllables which can be translated 'Hail, Śiva!' In the later development of Śaivism the pronunciation of these syllables was exalted into a primary religious duty. But in the creative period in which these hymns were written the name probably stood for the person, so that we have here a religious 'calling upon the name of

53 சொற்றுணைவேதியன்சோதிவானவன்
பொற்றுணை திருந்தடிபொருந்தக்கைதொழக்
கற்றுணைப்பூட்டியோர்கடலிற்பாய்ச்சினும்
நற்றுணையாவதுநமச்சிவாயவே.

54 பூவினுக்கருங்கலம்பொங்குதாமரை
யாவினுக்கருங்கலம் அரனஞ்சாடுதல்
கோவினுக்கருங்கலம்கோட்டமில்லது
நாவினுக்கருங்கலநமச்சிவாயவே.

55 வெந்தநீறருங்கலம்விரதிகட்கெலா
மந்தணர்க்கருங்கலமருமறையாறங்கங்
திங்களுக்கருங்கலந்திகழுநீண்முடி
நங்களுக்கருங்கலநமச்சிவாயவே.

the Lord' in the devotion of worship. In the first stanza there is a remarkable use of the term 'Word.' Modern Śaivites identify this 'Word' with Umā, Śiva's consort. We can compare the Sanskrit Vāk (Word) in the Ṛig Vēda.

The last lines of verse 53 are connected in the minds of Śaivites with a story that Apparswāmi was actually sunk in the sea by Jain persecutors, with two great stones tied to him, but on crying 'Hail, Śiva!' he floated to the surface.

The five products of the cow referred to in verse 54 are all used together in ceremonial purification—milk, curds, ghee, urine, and dung.

53. O Lord of Scripture, whom the Word doth help,
Celestial light of heaven, so I but praise,
With hands meetly upraised, Thy golden feet,
Then though men tie on me two weighty stones,
And sink me in the ocean's depth, e'en then
The cry 'Hail, Śiva,' would salvation be.

54. The lotus is the glory of all flowers;
The glory of all kine is Hara's use
Of that which they put forth. Glory of kings
Is the unswerving straightness of their deeds.
But if we ask the glory of the tongue,
'Tis to cry out aloud, 'Hail, Śiva, hail.'

55. For men who all renounce, 'tis glory true
To wear the sacred ash. For Brāhmans pure
The Vēdas and Vēdāṅgas are their pride.
The white moon's glory is to shine serene
On the long locks of Śiva, while for *us*
True glory is to cry 'Hail, Śiva, hail.'

56 கூற்றாயினவாறுவிலக்ககிலீர் கொடுமைபலசெய்
தனநானறியே
னேற்றாயடிக்கேயிரவும்பகலும் பிரியாதுவணங்கு
வனெப்பொழுதுந்
தோற்றாதென்வயிற்றினகம்படியே குடரோடுதொ
டக்கிமுடக்கியிட
ஆற்றேனடியேனதிகைக்கெடில வீரட்டானத்து
றையம்மானே.

57 மாதர்ப்பிறைக்கண்ணியானை மலையான்மகளொடும்
பாடிப்
போதொடுநீர்சுமந்தேத்திப்புகுவாரவர்பின்புகு
வேன்
யாதுஞ்சுவடுபடாமலையாறடைகின்றபோது
காதன்மடப்பிடியோடுங்களிறுவருவனகண்டேன்
கண்டேனவர்திருப்பாதங்கண்டறியாதனகண்
டேன்.

Tradition connects our next stanza with a story of Apparswāmi being smitten with an inward disease when he forsook Śaivism and became a Jain. The pain proved, says the legend, a convincing argument which reconverted him, whereupon he was promptly cured. But internal evidence proves this hymn to have been composed long after his return to Śaivism. Nandi is the name of Śiva's bull.

56. Thou takest not my deadly pain away,
My torments, Nandi-rider, never cease;
At Thy feet would I worship night and day,
But since my bowels writhe, and ne'er find peace,
I can no more! O Sire, to Thee I cry,
Who dwell'st by Keḍila, in Athihai.

---

Nature sometimes spoke to our author of God. The union of sexes even in animals one day spoke to him as a revelation of divine things.

57. I'll follow those who going to the shrine their praises sound,
With blooms and water for the god who wears the moon so mild
All lovely in His locks, a garland wreathed His neck around,
And with Him sing they Pārvati, the mountain god's fair child.
Once as I went to Aiyāṛu, with light and reverent tread,
I saw come two young elephants, male by loved female led,
And in that sight I saw God's foot, saw secret things unsaid.

58 நம்பனேயெங்கள்கோவேநாதனேயாதிமூர்த்தி
பங்கனேபரமயோகியென்றென்றேபரவிநாளுஞ்
செம்பொனேபவளக்குன்றேதிகழ்மலர்ப்பாதங்
காண்பா
னன்பனேயலைந்துபோனேனதிகைவீரட்டனாரே.

59 பண்ணினேர்மொழியாளுமைபங்கரோ
மண்ணினார்வலஞ்செய்மறைக்காடரோ
கண்ணினாலுமைக்காணக்கதவினைத்
திண்ணமாகத்திறந்தருள்செய்ம்மினே.

God is the great yogi, the wielder of mystic powers.

58. "O greatly loved, our King, our Lord, from all eternity,
Our portion, our true mystic," thus from day to day I sing.
O golden one, O hill of coral, I in love of Thee
Have wandered far and wide, Athihai Vīraṭṭānam's king,
Have wandered far the shining blossom of Thy foot to see.

---

One whole hymn, from which our next verse is taken, is a prayer for the opening of a door. Tradition has it that the great locked temple door at Vedārañyam swung open in answer to this song.

59. Umā is Thy portion, whose words are like song.
In fair Maṛaikkāḍu men circle round Thee
In worship. O graciously open this door
That we Thy true servants Thy glory may see.

---

Here is a very popular stanza. There used to be a beggar in Madras who recited it, and it alone, all day long.

60 அரியானையந்தணர்தஞ் சிந்தையானை
யருமறையி னகத்தானை யணுவையார்க்குந்
தெரியாததத்துவனைத் தேனைப்பாலைத்
திகழொளியைத்தேவர்கடங்கோனை மற்றைக்
கரியானை நான்முகனைக்கனலை க்காற்றைக்
கனைகடலைக்குலவரையைக்கலந்துநின்ற
பெரியானைப்பெரும்பற்றப்புலியூரானைப்
பேசாதநாளெல்லாம் பிறவாநாளே.

61 உழையுரித்த மானுரிதோலாடையானே
யுமையவடம்பெருமானே யிமையோரேறே
கழையிறுத்தகருங்கடனஞ்சுண்டகண்டா
கயிலாயமலையானேயுன்பாலன்பர்
பிழைபொறுத்தியென்பதுவும் பெரியோய்நின்றன்
கடனன்றே பேரருளுன் பாலதன்றே
அழையுறுத்து மாமயில்களாடுஞ்சோலை யாவடு
தண்டுறையுறையுமமரரேறே.

60. He is ever hard to find, but He lives in the thought
of the good;
He is the innermost secret of Scripture, inscrutable,
unknowable;
He is honey and milk and the shining light. He
is the king of the Devas,
Immanent in Vishṇu, in Brahmā, in flame and in
wind,
Yea in the mighty sounding sea and in the moun-
tains.
He is the great One who chooses Perumpattapuli-
yūr for His own.
If there be days when my tongue is dumb and
speaks not of Him,
Let no such days be counted in the record of my
life.

---

Whatever karma may teach of the inevitable consequence of evil, devotees hold that they may count on receiving divine forgiveness, for which the gracious nature of God is a sufficient pledge and guarantee.

61. Thy throat the black sea's poison drank, as 'twere
ambrosia sweet,
O deer-skin wearer, Umā's lord, king of the gods
on high;
Kailāsa's hill is Thine abode, and when Thy
lovers cry
"Forgive our sin," great One, forgiveness is Thy
duty meet;
For with Thee is great grace, lord of celestial
beings all,
Who dwell'st in Āvaḍuturai, where peacocks
dance and call.

62 திருக்கோயிலில்லாத திருவிலூருந்
திருவெண்ணீறணியாததிருவிலூரும்
பருக்கோடிப்பத்திமையாற் பாடாவூரும்
பாங்கினொடுபலதளிகளில்லாவூரும்
விருப்போடுவெண்சங்கமூதாவூரும்
விதானமும் வெண்கொடியுமில்லாவூரும்
அருப்போடு மலர்பறித்திட்டுண்ணாவூரும்
அவையெல்லாமூரல்லவடவிகாடே.

63 திருநாமமஞ்செழுத்துஞ் செப்பாராகிற்
றீவண்ணர் திறமொருகாற்பேசாராகில்
ஒருகாலுந்திருக்கோயில் சூழாராகில்
உண்பதன்முன் மலர்பறித்திட்டுண்ணாராகில்
அருநோய்கள்கெடவெண்ணீ றணியாராகி
லளியற்றார் பிறந்தவாறேதோவென்னிற்
பெருநோய்கண்மிகநலியப்பெயர்த்துஞ்செத்துப்
பிறப்பதற்கே தொழிலாகியிறக்கின்றாரே.

64 மக்களேமணந்ததாரமவ்வயிற்றவரை யோம்புஞ்
சிக்குளேயழுந்தியீசன் றிறம்படேன்றவமதோரேன்
கொப்புளேபோலத்தோன்றி யதனுளேமறையக்
கண்டு
மிக்களே பரத்தை யோம்ப வென்செய்வான் றோன்
றினேனே.

The dreadful fate in store for irreligious men that is of being slowly killed by sore sickness, then being born again to a joyless life that circles round once more to death in unending cycles of dreariness.

The 'letters five' in no. 63 refer to the five-syllabled phrase na-mah-Śi-vā-ya, whose praise is chanted in vv. 53-55.

62. The ill-starred town without a house of God,
  Wherein white ash on no man's brow doth glow,
The town where pious praises are unsung,
  Where are no wayside shrines men's faith to show,
Where none blow joyfully the conch-shell white,
  Where spread no canopies, no flags appear,
Where none make flowery offerings ere they eat,
  Call it no town, 'tis but a jungle drear.

63. If men speak not His name in letters five,
  Nor e'er the fire-formed Śiva's praise repeat,
And never walk in reverence round His shrine,
  And pluck no flowers for offering ere they eat,
If they for healing wear no sacred ash,
  I'll tell you whereunto such men were born,
'Twas that foul plagues might torture them to death,
  Then death bring rebirths endlessly forlorn.

---

Our last fragment from Apparswāmi is in the minor key, in which so many of his refrains are pitched. It seems to prove, contrary to tradition, that Appar was once a married man.

64. Immersed in painful cherishing
  Of child and wedded wife,
No room is there in me to feel
  Thy power, Lord of my life.
O whereunto came I to birth ?
  To cherish this false world ?
Or watch it, bubble-like, appear,
  Then be to nothing hurled ?

*(By permission of the Director, Colombo Museum)*

SUNDARAMŪRTI

# SUNDARAMŪRTI SWĀMI

AND HIS

# HYMNS

# III.

## SUNDARAMŪRTI SWĀMI

(Abbreviated as SUNDARAR)

THE third of these hymn-writers, named in full Sundaramūrti Swāmi, was, like Sambandar, a Brahman. He was born in the South Arcot District, and is generally believed to have flourished in the first quarter of the ninth century A.D. He evidently sat loose to caste scruples, for neither of his two wives was a Brahman. One was a dancing-girl in the Śaivite temple at Tiruvārūr, the modern Tiruvalur in the Tanjore District, while the other was a Vēḷāḷa woman of Tiruvottiyūr, now a suburb of Madras. His life seems to have been no happier than life in polygamy usually is, and to add to his difficulties he sometimes found himself without food for his ladies to eat. He frankly praised God for what he could get, and on the whole his hymns are on a lower spiritual plane than those of the first two writers, though there are some which bear the marks of real spiritual experience. Of the sixty-three saints whom Śaivites hold in special honour, Sundarar seems to have been the last, for he sang the praises of the other sixty-two.

65 நற்றமிழ்வல்ல ஞானசம்பந்த
னாவினுக்கரையனாளைப் போவானுங்
கற்றசூதனற்சாக்கியன்சிலந்தி
கண்ணப்பன்கணம்புல்லனென்றிவர்கள்
குற்றஞ்செய்யினுங்குணமெனக்கருதுங்
கொள்கை கண்டுநின்குரைகழலடைந்தேன்
பொற்றிரண்மணிக்கமலங்கள்மலரும்
பொய்கைசூழ்திருப்புன்கூருளானே.

66 பொன்னார்மேனியனே புலித்தோலையரைக்கசைத்து
மின்னார்செஞ்சடைமேல்மிளிர்கொன்றையணிந்த
வனே
மன்னேமாமணியேமழபாடியுண்மாணிக்கமே
யன்னேயுன்னையல்லாலினியாரைநினைக்கேனே.

Sundarar, as our first sample of him shews, was not only later than the two authors whom we have been studying; he was the last of the sixty-three canonized saints of Śaivism. A serious weakness of the religion here shews its head. Śiva has his favourites, who can do no wrong. The stanza is given in prose, for these names cannot fit into any English metrical line. The first two will be recognised as names of the poets whose work we have been considering. Nāḷaippōvān is Nandan, the pariah saint. Silandi (= spider) is Kōchchengaṭ Chola, who figures largely in early Tamil history.

65. Ñānasambandar and Tirunāvukkarasar, skilled in the Tamil tongue, Nāḷaippōvān, learned Sūdan, Sākkiyan, Silandi, Kaṇṇappan, Kaṇampullan, these may do wrong, but yet Thou count'st it right. Hence have I come to the sounding anklets of Thy feet, O lord of Tiruppungūr with its pools where blossoms many a golden lotus gem.

---

To English ears the metre of the next two verses, which are common favourites, has a curious sound. It is a close reproduction of the Tamil, so close that the tune of the Tamil hymn could be sung to the English words.

66. Golden art Thou in Thy form, girt around with the fierce tiger's skin,
Fair shines Thy tangle of hair, crowned with blooms from the kondai's bright tree,
Sov'reign, great jewel art Thou, the red ruby of Maḻapāḍi,
Mother, on Thee, none but Thee, can my heart evermore fixèd be.

67 கீளார்கோவணமுந்திருநீறுமெய்ப்பூசியுன்றன்
றாளேவந்தடைந்தேன்றலைவாவெனையேன்றுகொணீ
வாளார்கண்ணிபங்காமழபாடியுண்மாணிக்கமே
கேளாநின்னையல்லாலினியாரைநினைக்கேனே.

68 பத்திமையுமடிமையையுங்கைவிடுவான்பாவியேன்
பொத்தினநோயதுவிதனைப்பொருளறிந்தேன்
போய்த்தொழுவேன்
முத்தினைமாமணிதன்னைவயிரத்தைமூர்க்கனேன்
எத்தனைநாள்பிரிந்திருக்கேனென்னாரூரிறை
வனையே.

69 பித்தாபிறைசூடிபெருமானேயருளாளா
வெத்தான்மறவாதேநினைக்கின்றேன்மனத்துன்னை
வைத்தாய்பெண்ணைத்தென்பால்வெண்ணெய்நல்லூ
ரருட்டுறையு
ளத்தாவுனக்காளாயினியல்லேனெனலாமே.

67. Clad in the little loin-cloth, my body with holy ash white,
Lo I have come to Thy foot ; O my head, I beseech Thee, take me.
Portion of sword-eyed Umā, Thou red ruby of Maḻapāḍi,
Friend, 'tis on Thee, none but Thee, can my heart evermore fixèd be.

---

Is the Śiva manifested at one shrine so distinct from the Śiva manifested at another as to endanger the unity of God? If tradition is right, the danger is very real, for Sundarar was already worshipping at one shrine, Tiruvottiyūr, when he remembered the lord of Ārūr, and deciding to go to him like a returning prodigal, sang this stanza.

68. Ah sinful, I have left the path of love and service pure !
Now know I well the meaning of my sickness and my pain.
I will go worship. Fool ! how long can I so far remain
From Him, my pearl, my diamond rare, the king of great Ārūr.

---

The joy in God which shines in our next hymn evidently rests on some experience of divine grace which we should have liked to hear more definitely described.

69. O madman with the moon-crowned hair,
Thou lord of men, thou fount of grace,
How to forget Thee could I bear?
My soul hath aye for Thee a place.
Veṇṇey-nallūr, in "Grace's shrine"
South of the stream of Peṇṇai, there
My father, I became all thine ;
How could I now myself forswear?

70 நாயேன்பலநாளுநினைப்பின்றிமனத்துன்னைப்
பேயாய்த்திரிந்தெய்த்தேன்பெறலாகாவருள்பெற்
றேன்
வேயார்பெண்ணைத்தென்பால்வெண்ணெய்நல்லூர
ருட்டுறையு
ளாயாவுனக்காளாயினியல்லேனெனலாமே.

71 முடியேனினிப்பிறவேன்பெறின்மூவேன்பெற்ற
மூர்தீ
கொடியேன்பலபொய்யேயுரைப்பேனைக்குறிக்
கொண்ணீ
செடியார்பெண்ணைத்தென்பால்வெண்ணெய்நல்
லூரருட்டுறையு
ளடிகேளுனக்காளாயினியல்லேனெனலாமே.

72 மற்றுப்பற்றெனக்கின்றிநின்றிருப்பாதமேமனம்
பாவித்தேன்
பெற்றலும்பிறந்தேனினிப்பிறவாததன்மைவந்தெ
ய்தினேன்
கற்றவர்தொழுதேத்துஞ்சீர்க்கறையூரிற்பாண்டிக்
கொடுமுடி
நற்றவாவுனைநான்மறக்கினுஞ்சொல்லுநாநமச்சி
வாயவே.

70. I roamed, a cur, for many days
Without a single thought of Thee,
Roamed and grew weary, then such grace
As none could win Thou gavest me.
Veṇṇey-nallūr, in "Grace's shrine"
Where bamboos fringe the Peṇṇai, there
My Shepherd, I became all thine;
How could I now myself forswear?

71. Henceforth for me no birth, no death,
No creeping age, bull-rider mine.
Sinful and full of lying breath
Am I, but do Thou mark me Thine.
Veṇṇey-nallūr, in "Grace's shrine"
South of the wooded Peṇṇai, there
My Master, I became all thine;
How could I now myself forswear?

---

The varying mood of the saint, now joyous and triumphant, now plaintively looking for death, is reflected in the next two verses from one hymn.

72. Linked to naught else in life, my mind thinks only of Thy holy feet.
I'm born anew, from this time forth I pass the way of birth no more.
In Koḍumuḍi, lord austere, where wise men Thee with praises greet,
Should I forget Thee, my own tongue 'Hail, Śiva'! crying, would adore.

73 ஒவுநாளுணர்வழியுநாளுயிர்போகுநாளுயர்பாடை
மேற்
காவுநாளிவையென்றலாற்கருதேன்கிளர்புனற்கா
விரிப்
பாவுதண்புனல்வந்திழிபரஞ்சோதிபாண்டிக்கொ
டுமுடி
நாவலாவுனைநான்மறக்கினுஞ்சொல்லுநாநமச்சி
வாயவே.

74 அந்தணாளனுன் னடைக்கலம்புகுத
வவனைக் காப்பது காரணமாக
வந்தகாலன் றனாருயிரதனை
வவ்வினாய்க்குன்றன் வன்மைகண்டடியேன்
எந்தைநீயெனைநமன்றமர்நலியி
லிவன்மற்றென்னடியானென விலக்குஞ்
சிந்தையால்வந்துன்றிருவடியடைந்தேன்
செழும்பொழிற்றிருப்புன்கூருளானே.

73. When will the end draw nigh, sense fade, life
close, and I the bier ascend?
This, naught but this, is all my thought. But,
lord of speech, Thou light on high,
Where the bright streams of Kāviri to Koḍumuḍi
coolness lend,
Should I forget Thee, my own tongue to Thee
would loud 'Hail, Śiva' cry.

---

God should deliver His own from death. The appeal here is to the familiar story of Markandeya (see No. 3). Yama is the god of death who gathers in the souls of men.

74. The young saint refuge sought from Death;
To save him, Thou grim Death did'st slay,
Such deeds Thy might accomplisheth,
And I who have beheld them pray
"O Father, should dread Yama press
On me, forbid him. 'Tis my slave';
Do Thou in green Pungūr confess.
I've reached Thy foot, and Thou can'st save."

---

Sundarar is sure that Śiva will understand his perplexities in supplying the needs of his fair ladies. For does not Śiva Himself bear the burden of two ladies, Pārvati his consort, and Gangā (lady Ganges) in his hair? Sundarar, in the legend with which these verses are connected, when one of his wives was suffering hunger, miraculously received some uncooked rice from Siva. This was not enough; to complete the miracle Śiva must remove the rice for him to Ārūr the abode of his fair one. This too was done in answer to the hymn of which the next two stanzas are a sample.

75 நீளநினைந்தடியேனுமைநித்தலுங்கைதொழுவேன்
வாளனகண்மடவாளவள்வாடிவருந்தாமே
கோளிலியெம்பெருமான்குண்டையூர்ச்சிலநெல்லு
ப்பெற்றே
னாளிலையெம்பெருமானவையட்டித்தரப்பணியே.

76 பாதியோர்பெண்ணைவைத்தாய்படருஞ்சடைக்கங்
கைவைத்தாய்
மாதர்நல்லார்வருத்தமதுநீயுமறிதியன்றே
கோதில்பொழில்புடைசூழ்குண்டையூர்ச்சிலநெல்
லுப்பெற்றே
னாதியேயற்புதனேயவையட்டித்தரப்பணியே.

77 தம்மையேபுகழ்ந்திச்சைபேசினுஞ்சார்வினுந்
தொண்டர்தருகிலாப்
பொய்ம்மையாளரைப்பாடாதேயெந்தைபுகலூர்பா
டுமின்புலவீர்கா
ளிம்மையேதருஞ்சோறுங்கூறையுமேத்தலாமிடர்
கெடலுமாம்
அம்மையேசிவலோகமாள்வதற்கியாதுமையுற
வில்லையே.

75. Ever I think but of Thee;
Daily in worship I bow;
She of the sword-piercing eyes,
Leave her not suffering now.
Kōḷili's lord, Thou didst give
Rice in Kuṇḍaiyūr this day.
No man to bring it have I,
Bid it be sent me, I pray.

76. Thou art half woman Thyself;
Gaṅgā is in Thy long hair.
Full well canst Thou comprehend
Burden of women so fair.
Kuṇḍaiyūr circled with gems,
There didst Thou give rice to-day.
Source of all, wonderful one,
Bid it be sent me, I pray.

---

The saint advises his fellow-poets to sing the praises of Śiva rather than the praises of men because they seldom reward the poets. Śiva rewards them here and hereafter. The Pāri mentioned in 78 was a chieftain in the Tamil country in the early centuries of our era, famed for his liberality.

77. Though ye fawn on men of lies,
They to saints will nothing give;
Sing not them, O poets wise,
But if ye would wealth receive
Sing the Sire of Puhalūr;
Here your wants will be supplied,
Pain will flee; there evermore
Ye will kings in heav'n abide.

78 மிடுக்கிலாதானைவீமனேவிறல்விசயனேவில்லுக்கிவனென்று
கொடுக்கிலாதானைப்பாரியேயென்றுகூறினுங்கொடுப்பாரிலை
பொடிக்கொள்மேனியெம்புண்ணியன்புகலூரைப்பாடுமின்புலவீர்கா
அடுக்குமேலமருலகமாள்வதற்கியாதுமையுறவில்லையே.

79 வாழ்வாவது மாயம்மிது மண்ணாவது திண்ணம்
பாழ்போவதுபிறவிக்கடல்பசிநோய்செய்தபறிதான்
றாழாதறஞ் செய்ம்மின்றடங்கண்ணான்மல ரோனுங்
கீழ்மேலுற நின்றான்றிருக் கேதாரமெ னீரே.

78. Call the weak by Bhīma's name,
    Style him Arjun with his bow,
Give the mean man Pāri's fame,
    Not a gift will he bestow.
Sing, O bards, our holy God,
    White with ash, in Puhalūr.
In the deathless one's abode
    Ye shall reign for evermore.

---

Life and experience have no value, no reality. God alone is real, the refuge from the unreal.

79. Our life is all unreal,
    Its end is only dust,
Out of the sea of birth
    Come ruin, pain and lust.
Delay not to do good
    But praise Ketāram's king,
Whom Vishṇu and great Brahm
    Vainly sought sorrowing.

*(By permission of the Director, Colombo Museum)*

MĀṆIKKA VĀSAHAR

# MĀNIKKA VĀSAHAR

AND HIS

# HYMNS

## IV.

# MĀNIKKA VĀSAHAR

(Sanskrit form MĀṆIKYA VĀCHAKA)

IN the days when the powerful Pāndyan Kings flourished in Madura, there was once a prime minister who early became convinced of the transitoriness of this world's life and its riches. When on a visit to Perundurai, now Āvudaiyārkoil in the Tanjore District, he suddenly and completely came under the influence of a Brahman religious teacher, who for him was the manifestation of the very God Himself. Then and there he began to sing the "Sacred Utterance" (Tiruvāsaham), and was named by his preceptor "Utterer of Jewels" (Māṇikka Vāsahar). Returning to Madura, he forsook his high office with all its rewards, to become a religious poet wandering without earthly attachments from shrine to shrine. The stories clustering around his religious experience can be read by English readers in Dr. Pope's great edition of his work. We find him practising austerities at Chidambaram, or miraculously giving the gift of speech to the dumb daughter of the Chōḻa king, or defeating in disputation a band of Buddhists from Ceylon, but of certain historical information about him we have practically none. Even the question of the century in which he lived is a battleground of the antiquarians. Tradition places him in the fifth century, earlier than the writers of the Dēvāram;

but the opinion of scholars seems to be converging on the view that he lived in the latter half of the ninth, or the first half of the tenth century of our era. Another of his works is the Tirukkōvaiyār, an erotic poem of four hundred stanzas. Among Tamil Śaivite writers none makes a stronger devotional appeal than Māṇikka Vāsahar. There is a common Tamil saying that nothing can melt the heart of the man who is not melted by the Tiruvāsaham.

80 மெய்தா னரும்பி விதிர்விதிர்த் துன்விரை யார்கழற்கென்
கைதான் றலைவைத்துக் கண்ணீர் ததும்பி வெதும்பியுள்ளம்
பொய்தான் றவிர்ந்துன்னைப் போற்றி சயசய போற்றியென்னுங்
கைதா னெகிழ விடேனுடை யாயென்னைக் கண்டுகொள்ளே.

81 கொள்ளேன் புரந்தரன் மாலயன் வாழ்வு குடிகெடினு
நள்ளே னினதடி யாரொடல் லானர கம்புகினு
மெள்ளேன் றிருவரு ளாலே யிருக்கப் பெறினிறைவா
வுள்ளேன் பிறதெய்வ முன்னையல் லாதெங்க ளுத்தமனே.

82 நாடகத்தா லுன்னடியார் போனடித்து நானடுவே
வீடகத்தே புகுந்திடுவான் மிகப்பெரிதும் விரைகின்றேன்
ஆடகச்சீர் மணிக்குன்றே யிடையறா வன்புனக்கென்
னூடகத்தே நின்றுருகத் தந்தருளெம் முடையானே.

Stanzas 80-92 are samples from an opening poem of one hundred stanzas, each ten of which has its own metre and is fairly complete in itself. They fairly reflect the saint's varying moods. Notice the importance he attaches to emotion; his worst self-reproach is for feeling no frenzy. As to his conception of God, see how the word 'grace' recurs in nearly every stanza. And yet that God of grace is called (in No. 84) both being and non-existence.

### THE HUNDRED VERSES

80. Thrills and trembles my frame;
 Hands are lifted on high;
Here at Thy fragrant feet,
 Sobbing and weeping I cry;
Falsehood forsaking, I shout,
 "Victory, victory, praise!"
Lord of my life, these clasped hands
 Worship shall bring Thee always.

81. Indra or Vishṇu or Brahm,
 Their divine bliss crave not I;
I seek the love of Thy saints,
 Though my house perish thereby.
To the worst hell I will go,
 So but Thy grace be with me.
Best of all, how could my heart
 Think of a god beside Thee?

---

82. Though like Thy saints I seem, 'tis but the acting of a part.
Yet wondrous swift I run to reach the heaven where Thou art.
O hill of gold and precious gems, grant in Thy grace to me
A heart to melt, lord of my life, in ceaseless love to Thee.

83 யானேதும் பிறப்பஞ்சேனிறப்பதனுக் கென்
கடவேன்
வானேயும் பெறில்வேண்டேன் மண்ணாள்வான்
மதித்துமிரேன்
றேனேயு மலர்க்கொன்றைச் சிவனேயெம் பெரு
மானெம்
மானேயுன் னருள்பெறுநா ளென்றென்றே
வருந்துவனே.

84 வானாகி மண்ணாகி வளியாகி யொளியாகி
யூனாகி யுயிராகி யுண்மையுமா யின்மையுமாய்க்
கோனாகி யானெனதென் றவரவரைக் கூத்தாட்டு
வானாகி நின்றாயை யென்சொல்லி வாழ்த்துவனே.

85 வெள்ளந்தாழ் விரிசடையாய் விடையாய் விண்
ணோர்
பெருமானேயெனக்கேட்டுவேட்டநெஞ்சாய்ப்
பள்ளந்தா ழுறுபுனலிற் கீழ்மே லாகப்
பதைத்துருகு மவர்நிற்க வென்னை யாண்டாய்க்
குள்ளந்தா னின்றுச்சி யளவு நெஞ்சா
யுருகாதா லுடம்பெல்லாங் கண்ணா யண்ணா
வெள்ளந்தான் பாயாதா னெஞ்சங் கல்லாங்
கண்ணிணையு மரமாந்தீ வினையி னேற்கே.

83. I have no fear of births, but quake at thought that
I must die.
E'en heav'n to me were naught; for earth's whole
empire what care I?
O Śiva wreathed with honeyed blossoms, "When
shall come the morn
When Thou wilt grant Thy grace to me?" I cry
with anguish torn.

84. The sky, earth, wind, the light, our very flesh and
life art Thou,
Being art Thou, non-being too, Thou king, who
see'st how
Men dance like puppets with their foolish thoughts
of 'I' and 'Mine,'
While Thou the cords dost pull. What words can
tell Thy praise divine?

---

85. At sound of cries like this, "O Bull-rider whose
spreading hair
The falling stream receives! Heaven's Lord," true
devotees there were,
Whose love-thrilled heart broke forth, like stopped-
up rivers rushing down.
Yet Thou didst choose no one of them, but me to
be Thine own.
And yet my body will not turn from heel to head
one heart
To melt in love for Thee, one eye to shed the tears
that smart
In swelling floods. Ah! wretched that I am, who
only moan!
My two eyes are unfeeling wood, my heart a great
dead stone!

86 வினையிலே கிடந்தேனைப் புகுந்து நின்று
போதுநான் வினைக்கேட னென்பாய் போல
வினையனா னென்றுன்னை யறிவித் தென்னை
யாட்கொண்டெம் பிரானானாய்க் கிரும்பின் பாவை
யனையநான் பாடேனின் றாடே னந்தோ
வலறிடே னுலறிடே னாவி சோரேன்
முனைவனே முறையோநா னான வாறு
முடிவறியேன் முதலந்த மாயினானே.

87 கேட்டாரு மறியாதான் கேடொன் றில்லான்
கிளையிலான் கேளாதே யெல்லாங் கேட்டா
னாட்டார்கள் விழித்திருப்ப ஞாலத் துள்ளே
நாயினுக்குத் தவிசிட்டு நாயி னேற்கே
காட்டா தனவெல்லாங் காட்டிப் பின்னுங்
கேளா தனவெல்லாங் கேட்பித் தென்னை
மீட்டேயும் பிறவாமற் காத்தாட் கொண்டா
னெம்பெருமான் செய்திட்ட விச்சை தானே.

88 தேவர்கோ வறியாத தேவ தேவன்
செழும்பொழில்கள் பயந்துகாத் தழிக்கு மற்றை
மூவர்கோ னாய்நின்ற முதல்வன் மூர்த்தி
மூதாதை மாதாளும் பாகத் தெந்தை

86. Amid the fruits of deeds I lay. Thou didst thyself reveal
With words of comfort saying "Come, I will destruction deal
To evil fruit of deeds," and thus thou mad'st me all Thy slave.
And yet I stand as if a statue made of steel, nor rave,
Nor sing, nor cry, nor wail—woe's me—nor in my spirit faint
With deep desire, so dull am I. O being ancient,
Thou art beginning, Thou art end: tell me, how can I be
So dead at heart? The end of this I do not dare to see.

---

87. Him though men seek, none fully know; in Him no evil is.
None are His kindred; knowledge perfect, effortless is His.
A cur am I, yet He hath giv'n to me in sight of men
A place on earth, and shewed me things far beyond mortal ken.
He told me what no ears can hear; from future births He sav'd.
Such magic wrought my Lord who me hath lovingly enslaved.

88. Our God of gods, whom e'en the devas' king knows but in part,
Ruleth the three who in the fair world-gardens life impart,
And life maintain, and life destroy; our First, Reality,
Father of old, whose consort Umā is, our sovereign, He

யாவர்கோ னென்னையும்வந் தாண்டு கொண்டான்
யாமார்க்குங் குடியல்லோம் யாது மஞ்சோ
மேவினோ மவனடியா ரடியா ரோடு
மேன்மேலுங் குடைந்தாடி யாடு வோமே.

89 செய்வ தறியாச் சிறுநாயேன் செம்பொற் பாத
மலர்காணாப்
பொய்யர் பெறும்பே றத்தனையும் பெறுதற் குரி
யேன் பொய்யிலா
மெய்யர் வெறியார் மலர்ப்பாத மேவக் கண்டுங்
கேட்டிருந்தும்
பொய்ய னேனா னுண்டுடுத்திங் கிருப்ப தானேன்
போரேறே

90 இழித்தன னென்னை யானே யெம்பிரான் போற்றி
போற்றி
பழித்திலே னுன்னை யென்னை யாளுடைப்பாதம்
போற்றி
பிழைத்தவை பொறுக்கை யெல்லாம் பெரியவர்
கடமை போற்றி
யொழித்திடிவ் வாழ்வு போற்றி யும்பர்நாட் டெம்
பிரானே.

Came down in grace and made e'en me to be His very own.
Henceforth before no man I bow; I fear but Him alone.
Now of His servants' servants I have joined the sacred throng,
And ever more and more I'll bathe in bliss, with dance and song.

89. The meanest cur am I; I know not how to do the right;
'Twere but what I deserve, should'st Thou my wickedness requite
With the dread fate of those who never saw Thy flowery feet;
For though mine eyes have seen, my ears have heard saints guileless, meet,
Who reached Thy fragrant presence, yet I stay, for false am I,
Fit for naught save to eat and dress, Lion of victory.

---

90. None but myself has sunk myself. Thy name be ever praised!
No blame lay I on Thee, lauds to my Master be upraised!
Yet to forgive is aye a mark of greatness. Praise to Thee!
Lord of the land celestial, Praise! O end this life for me.

91 மானேர் நோக்கி யுடையாள் பங்கா மறையீ றறியா
மறையோனே
தேனே யமுதே சிந்தைக் கரியாய் சிறியேன் பிழை
பொறுக்குங்
கோனே சிறிதே கொடுமை பறைந்தேன் சிவமா
நகர்குறுகப்
போனு ரடியார் யானும் பொய்யும் புறமே போந்
தோமே.

92 யானே பொய்யென் னெஞ்சும் பொய்யென்
னன்பும்பொய்
ஆனல் வினையே னழுதா லுன்னைப் பெறலாமே
தேனே யமுதே கரும்பின் றெளிவே தித்திக்கு
மானே யருளா யடியே னுனைவந் துறுமாறே.

93 விச்ச தின்றியே விளைவு செய்குவாய்
விண்ணு மண்ணக முழுதும் யாவையும்
வைச்சு வாங்குவாய் வஞ்ச கப்பெரும்
புலைய னேனையுன் கோயில் வாயிலிற்
பிச்ச னாக்கினாய் பெரிய வன்பருக்
குரிய னாக்கினாய் தாம்வ ளர்த்ததோர்
நச்சு மாமர மாயி னுங்கொலார்
நானு மங்ஙனே யுடைய நாதனே.

91. The fawn-eyed maid is part of Thee! From holy writ Thou'rt hid!
Thou'rt honey, yea ambrosia, by man's mind not compassèd.
O king who bearest with my faults, some harsh words did I say.
Thy saints have entered heaven. Without, falsehood and I still stay.

92. Since I am false, and false my heart, and false my very love,
Howe'er I weep, still held by deeds, can I reach Thee above?
O honey, nectar, O essential sweetness, great as sweet,
Grant grace to me to find the path that leads unto Thy feet.

93. Heav'n, earth, and all that therein is, thou makest without seed.
Thou dost preserve and Thou destroy. 'Tis Thou who hast decreed
That I though treacherous, mean, should be a man who frenzied faints
Before Thy temple gates, one with the band of Thy true saints.
What men themselves have planted, e'en a poisonous mango tree,
They root not up. O Lord of mine, as such a tree keep me.

---

Our next five stanzas, taken from a hymn of fifty, are full of the pathos expressed in the title, which is a refrain recurring in every verse. Only flashes of the light of the presence of God pierce the prevailing gloom. The saint cannot free himself from sensuality,

94 கடையவனேனைக்கருணையினாற்கலந்தாண்டு
கொண்ட
விடையவனேவிட்டிடுதிகண்டாய்விறல்வேங்கை
யின்றோ
லுடையவனேமன்னுமுத்தரகோசமங்கைக்கரசே
சடையவனேதளர்ந்தேனெம்பிரா னென்னைத்தாங்
கிக்கொள்ளே.

95 காருறுகண்ணியரைம்புலனாற்றங்கரைமரமாய்
வேருறுவேனைவிடுதிகண்டாய்விளங்குந்திருவா
ரூருறைவாய்மன்னுமுத்தரகோசமங்கைக்கரசே
வாருறுபூண்முலையாள்பங்கவென்னைவளர்ப்பவனே.

96 மறுத்தனன்யானுன்னருளறியாமையிலென்ம
ணியே
வெறுத்தெனைநீவிட்டிடுதிகண்டாய்வினையின்றொ
குதி
யொறுத்தெனையாண்டுகொளுத்தரகோசமங்கைக்
கரசே
பொறுப்பரன்றேபெரியோர்சிறுநாய்கடம்பொய்
யினையே.

even while he hates it. He wonders whether even the God who drank poison for others' sake will leave him alone.

### Wilt Thou Leave Me?

94. Mingling in grace with me, O rider of the bull,
Thou mad'st me Thine.
But wilt Thou leave me? Thou whose form in the fierce tiger's skin is clad,
Uttarakōsamaṅgai old has Thee for king. O lord of mine
With matted hair, hold Thou me up; for I am weary grown and sad.

95. Set in the marge of flowing stream that eats its banks away, the tree
Shakes to its fall; and thus am I, my sense bewitch'd by maids' dark eyes.
Uttarakōsamaṅgai's king, spouse of gem-vested Pārvati,
Who dwell'st in Ārūr holy, O protector, for my help arise.

96. In ignorance I spurned thy grace. Dost Thou, my gem, now me despise,
And wilt thou leave me? O destroy my sum of deeds and make me thine.
Uttarakōsamaṅgai's king, 'tis surely true, the great and wise,
When only little curs play false, to mercy ever will incline.

97 என்னையப்பாவஞ்சலென்பவரின்றிநின்றெய்த்த
லைந்தேன்
மின்னையொப்பாய்விட்டிடுதிகண்டாயுவமிக்கின்
மெய்யே
யுன்னையொப்பாய் மன்னுமுத்தரகோசமங்கைக்
கரசே
யன்னையொப்பாயெனக்கத்தனொப்பாயென்னரும்
பொருளே.

98 ஏசினும்யானுன்னையேத்தினுமென்பிழைக்கேகு
ழைந்து
வேசறுவேனைவிடுதிகண்டாய்செம்பவளவெற்பிற்
றேசுடையாயென்னையாளுடையாய்சிற்றுயிர்க்கி
ரங்கிக்
காய்சினவாலமுண்டாயமுதுண்ணக்கடையவனே.

97. With none to cheer me from my fear, far have I wandered wearily,
O Lightning-like, and wilt Thou leave me? If I truly thee compare,
Uttarakōsamaṅgai's king, I find naught else resembling Thee;
But a true father, mother dear art Thou to me, my treasure rare.

98. Whether I praise or curse Thee, still I'm stained with sin and sorrowing.
Yet, wilt Thou leave me? Splendour shining like the red-hued coral mount,
Master, thou drankest poison black, the humbler beings pitying,
That I, Thy meanest one, might find no poison, but a nectar fount.

---

Our poet made songs which maidens might sing in their rhythmical games, or as they sat at the grinding-stone. In India the boatman sings as he rows, the ryot sings as he draws from the well, the sepoy sings on his march. A feature of such songs is the refrain, which is usually a mere collection of euphonic syllables, though it may have a meaning. Here are specimens of a few songs intended for women. The refrain of the first, "Ēlōrembāvāy" probably means "Receive and ponder what I say, O lady." The Grinding song, strangely enough, is used at funerals, as also is the 'Antiphony.' The song of 'The Three Castles' Destruction' is supposed to accompany play with a ball or a kind of shuttle called 'undī.' For the legend of the Three Castles, see page 7. 'The Shoulder-Play' is for some ancient game in which women grasped each other's shoulders.

99 முன்னைப்பழம்பொருட்குமுன்னைப்பழம்பொ
ருளே
பின்னைப்புதுமைக்கும்பேர்த்துமப்பெற்றியனே
யுன்னைப்பிரானாகப்பெற்றவுன்சீரடியோ
முன்னடியார்தாள்பணிவோமாங்கவர்க்கேபாங்
காவோம்
அன்னவரேயெங்கணவராவாரவருகந்து
சொன்னபரிசேதொழும்பாய்ப்பணிசெய்வோம்
இன்னவகையே யெமக்கெங்கோனல்குதியேல்
என்னகுறையுமிலோமேலோரெம்பாவாய்.

100 உங்கையிற்பிள்ளையுனக்கேயடைக்கலமென்
றங்கப்பழஞ்சொற்புதுக்குமெம்மச்சத்தா
லெங்கள்பெருமானுனக்கொன்றுரைப்போங்கே
ளெங்கொங்கைநின்னன்பரல்லார்தோள்சேரற்க
வெங்கையுனக்கல்லாதெப்பணியுஞ்செய்யற்க
கங்குல்பகலெங்கண்மற்றொன்றுங்காணற்க
விங்கிப்பரிசேயெமக்கெங்கோனல்குதியே
லெங்கெழிலென்ஞாயிறெமக்கேலோரெம்பா
வாய்.

101 வேதமும்வேள்வியுமாயினார்க்கு
மெய்ம்மையும்பொய்ம்மையுமாயினார்க்குச்
சோதியுமாயிருளாயினார்க்குத்
துன்பமுமாயின்பமாயினார்க்குப்
பாதியுமாய்முற்றுமாயினார்க்குப்
பந்தமுமாய்வீடுமாயினாருக்
காதியுமந்தமுமாயினாருக்
காடப்பொற்சுண்ணமிடித்துநாமே.

## Song of The Maidens

99. Older are Thou than the oldest of all,
Newest of all that is new.
At Thy saints' feet we in service will fall,
We are Thy handmaidens true.
None but Thy bondsmen shall call us their own;
Lord, we would none others wed;
We would be slaves at their bidding alone:
So be our bliss perfected.
Ēlōrembāvāy.

100. "Sure for Thy child there is refuge with Thee,"
Trembling we take up the cry.
Hear, O our Lord, while we bring Thee one plea,
Grant but one boon for our joy.
May only Thy lovers rest on our breast,
Let our hands' labour be theirs.
Only on such our eyes night and day rest,
Then sun rise west, east, who cares?
Elōrembāvāy.

## The Grinding Song

101. Grind we the powder gold, that He may bathe;
For He is Scripture, He is sacrifice;
He's being's truth, and being's falsehood too;
Light is He, yea, and He is darkness deep;
He is deep sorrow, and true bliss is He;
He is the half, and He again the whole;
Bondage is He, but He is true release;
He is the alpha, He the omega.

102 பூசுவதும்வெண்ணீறுபூண்பதுவும்பொங்கரவம்
பேசுவதுந்திருவாயான்மறைபோலுங்காணேடீ
பூசுவதும்பேசுவதும்பூண்பதுவுங்கொண்டென்னை
யீசனவனெவ்வுயிர்க்குமியல்பானான்சாழலோ.

103 என்னப்பனெம்பிரானெல்லார்க்குந்தானீசன்
றுன்னம்பெய்கோவணமாக்கொள்ளுமதுவென்
னேடீ
மன்னுகலைதுன்னுபொருண்மறைநான்கேவான்ச
ரடாத்
தன்னையேகோவணமாச்சாத்தினன்காண்சாழலோ.

104 கோயில்சுடுகாடுகொல்புலித்தோனல்லாடை
தாயுமிலிதந்தையிலிதான்றனியன்காணேடீ
தாயுமிலிதந்தையிலிதான்றனியனாயிடினுங்
காயிலுலகனைத்துங்கற்பொடிகாண்சாழலோ.

105 தானந்தமில்லான்றனையடைந்தநாயேனை
யானந்தவெள்ளத்தழுத்துவித்தான்காணேடீ
யானந்தவெள்ளத்தழுத்துவித்ததிருவடிகள்
வானுந்துதேவர்கட்கோர்வான்பொருள்காண்சா
ழலோ.

## Śiva's Mysteries (An Antiphony)

102. "His form is smeared with ashes white; the snake His strange adornment is;
The secret scriptures utters He: what kind of god, my friend, is this?"
"Why talk of ash-smear, holy speech, adornment strange? This only know,
This god, of every living thing is the true nature. Chāḷalō."

103. "My father and my master, He of all men Lord supreme, is clad
With but a hanging loin-cloth stitched; pray tell me, friend, is He not mad?"
"The Vedas four with meaning fraught, the everlasting Śāstras, know
That these are but the threads whereof is wove His loin-cloth. Chāḷalō."

104. "The burning-ground's His temple fine; the tiger's skin His raiment is;
Father or mother hath He none; He's all alone; my friend, see this."
"Though He no parents hath, no kin, yet should His anger kindle, lo,
The whole wide world would straightway turn to dust and ashes. Chāḷalō."

105. "Though I am but a cur, yet when I turned to Him who hath no end,
Into a sea of bliss He made me sink o'erwhelmed; see this, my friend."
"Those holy feet that sank thee in the sea of bliss o'erwhelmèd, know,
E'en to the very gods in heav'n they're richest treasure. Chāḷalō."

106 வளைந்ததுவில்லுவிளைந்ததுபூச
லுளைந்தனமுப்புரமுந்தீபற
வொருங்குடன்வெந்தவாறுந்தீபற.

107 ஈரம்புகண்டிலமேகம்பர்தங்கையி
லோரம்பேமுப்புரமுந்தீபற
வொன்றும்பெருமிகையுந்தீபற.

108 தச்சுவிடுத்தலுந்தாமடியிட்டலு
மச்சுமுறிந்ததென்றுந்தீபற
வழிந்தனமுப்புரமுந்தீபற.

109 ஏழைத்தொழும்பனேனெத்தனையோகாலமெல்
லாம்
பாழுக்கிறைத்தேன்பரம்பரனைப்பணியாதே
யூழிமுதற்சிந்தாதநன்மணிவந்தென்பிறவித்
தாழைப்பறித்தவாதோணோக்கமாடாமோ.

### The Three Castles' Destruction

106. Bent was the bow, begun the fight,
The castles three were 'whelmèd quite, (Fly, undī)
Three castles blazing with one light. (Fly, undī)

107. One bolt in Śiva's hand saw we,
One single bolt for castles three, (Fly, undī)
And e'en that one scarce needed He. (Fly, undī)

108. Cleft lay the car at His foot's tread,
The axle was all shatterèd, (Fly, undī)
Three castles ruined lay and dead. (Fly, undī)

### The Shoulder-Play

109. Poor slave was I, how long I poured out all my days for naught,
To Him the all-supreme no homage rendering! Yet see,
How He, the jewel from eternal ages incorrupt,
Has come and drawn the prison-bolt of births, and set me free.
Play we Tōṇōkkam

---

In the poetry of all lands lovers have appealed to birds to be their messengers to the distant loved one. This is so common in Indian poetry as to have become a recognised convention. Here the saint sends his message of love and devotion, in one case by a humming bee, in the other by the Indian cuckoo, to Śiva who dwells in Tillai, *i.e.* Chidambaram.

110 வன்னெஞ்சக்கள்வன்மனவலியனென்னாதே
கன்னெஞ்சுருக்கிக்கருணையினாலாண்டுகொ
ண்ட
வன்னந்திளைக்குமணிதில்லையம்பலவன்
பொன்னங்கழலுக்கேசென்றூதாய்கோத்
தும்பீ.

111 நாயேனைத்தன்னடிகள்பாடுவித்தநாயகனைப்
பேயேனதுள்ளப்பிழைபொறுக்கும்பெருமை
யனைச்
சீயேதுமில்லாதென்செய்பணிகள்கொண்டரு
ளுந்
தாயானவீசற்கேசென்றூதாய்கோத்தும்பீ.

112 நானுமென்சிந்தையுநாயகனுக்கெவ்விடத்தோந்
தானுந்தன்றையலுந்தாழ்சடையோனாண்டில
னேல்
வானுந்திசைகளுமாகடலுமாயபிரான்
றேனுந்துசேவடிக்கேசென்றூதாய்கோத்தும்பீ.

113 பொய்யாயசெல்வத்தேபுக்கழுந்திநாடோறு
மெய்யாக்கருதிக்கிடந்தேனையாட்கொண்ட
வையாவென்னாருயிரேயம்பலவாவென்றவன்
றன்
செய்யார்மலரடிக்கேசென்றூதாய்கோத்தும்பீ.

### The Bee's Message

110. Hard-hearted thief, stiff-necked was I, but no such name He called me ;
My stony heart He melted, and by mercy He enthralled me.
The swans abound in Tillai's lovely hall of gold, His dwelling.
Fly, king of bees, at His gold anklets hum, my message telling.

111. Cur though I am, my lord has set me His great glory singing ;
To me, the mad, His patient grace is aye forgiveness bringing ;
Scorning me not, He deigns to take the service I can do Him.
Mother and God. Go, king of bees, hum thou my message to Him.

112. Far would my heart and mind have gone from Him, but He compelled me,
The lord with tangled locks, and His fair spouse, they saved and held me.
He is the sky, the mighty sea, east, west, north, south, indwelling.
His feet with honey drop. There, king of bees, my praise be telling.

113. In this world's treasure false immersed lay I, and self-deceivèd,
Held it for treasure true, but for His own He me receivèd.
My precious life itself is He, in Tillai's hall abiding.
Go, king of bees, at His red lotus feet my words confiding.

114 தேன்பழச்சோலைபயிலுஞ்சிறுகுயிலேயிது
கேணீ
வான்பழித்திம்மண்புகுந்துமனிதரையாட்கொ
ண்டவள்ள
லூன்பழித்துள்ளம்புகுந்தென்னுணர்வதுவாய
வொருத்தன்
மான்பழித்தாண்டமென்னோக்கிமணாளனைநீவ
ரக்கூவாய்.

115 போற்றியென்வாழ்முதலாகியபொருளே
புலர்ந்ததுபூங்கழற்கிணைதுணைமலர்கொண்
டேத்திநின்றிருமுகத்தெமக்கருண்மலரு
மெழினகைகொண்டுநின்றிருவடிதொழுகோஞ்
சேற்றிதழ்க்கமலங்கண்மலருந்தண்வயல்சூழ்
திருப்பெருந்துறையுறைசிவபெருமானே
யேற்றுயர்கொடியுடையாயெனையுடையா
யெம்பெருமான்பள்ளியெழுந்தருளாயே.

### THE CUCKOO'S ERRAND

114. Hear, little cuckoo in the honey'd orchard groves.
Heav'n did He spurn ; to save us men, to earth He came,
Boundless in giving, recking naught of flesh of mine,
Entered my mind, and there my very thought became.
He, the alone, the spouse of her whose pure eye's ray
Shames the gazelle in softness, call Him hither, pray.

---

One of the little childishnesses involved in idolatry is that every morning with solemn ceremony the idol must be wakened from his sleep, bathed, and dressed. Here is a song with which he is roused from slumber. But notice how successfully our author has filled his poem with the fresh morning feeling, and the sights and sounds of the sudden break of the Indian dawn.

### THE IDOL'S AWAKENING

115. Hail to Thee, treasure rare,
Source of all prosperity,
Dawn has come, at Thy feet,
Flowers themselves, fair flowers lay we.
Praising Thee, we await
Smiles that blossom fair and sweet
In Thy face, as we fall
Prone adoring at Thy feet.

Śiva, Lord, dweller in
Perundurai, where expand
Lotus flowers, petalled white,
In the cool moist pasture land,
Thou whose flag is the bull,
Thou the Lord of all my ways,
Now O Lord of us all,
From Thy couch rise in Thy grace.

116 அருணனிந்திரன்றிசையணுகினனிருள்போ
யகன்றதுவுதயநின்மலர்த்திருமுகத்தின்
கருணையின்சூரியனெழவெழநயனக்
கடிமலர்மலரமற்றண்ணலங்கண்ணாந்
திரணிரையறுபதமுரல்வனவிவையோர்
திருப்பெருந்துறையுறைசிவபெருமானே
யருணிதிதரவருமானந்தமலையே
யலைகடலேபள்ளியெழுந்தருளாயே.

117 கூவினபூங்குயில்கூவினகோழி
குருகுகளியம்பினவியம்பினசங்க
மோவினதாரகையொளியொளியுதயத்
தொருப்படுகின்றதுவிருப்பொடுநமக்குத்
தேவநற்செறிகழற்றாளிணைகாட்டாய்
திருப்பெருந்துறையுறைசிவபெருமானே
யாவருமறிவரியாயெமக்கெளியா
யெம்பெருமான்பள்ளியெழுந்தருளாயே.

116. Now anigh Indra's East
Draws the sun; dark flies apace
At the dawn; and the sun
Of the kindness in Thy face
Riseth high'r, ever high'r,
As like fair flowers opening,
Eyes unclose from their sleep,
Eyes of Thee our beauteous king.

Hear how now clouds of bees
Humming bright fill all the air.
Śiva, Lord, dweller in
Holy Perunduṛai fair,
Thou wilt come to bestow
Favours rich, Oh shew Thy face!
Mountain-joy, ocean-bliss,
From Thy couch rise in Thy grace.

117. Cocks now crow to the morn,
While the cuckoos loudly call;
Little birds sweetly sing,
And the conch-shell sounds o'er all;
Light of stars fades away
Into common light of day;
Dawn and sun come as one,
Now to us, O God, display

In Thy love Thy twin feet,
Gracious, decked with anklets rare.
Śiva, Lord, dweller in holy Perunduṛai fair,
Hard for all men to find,
Yet to me Thou shewedst Thy face.
Now O Lord of us all,
From Thy couch rise in Thy grace.

118 இன்னிசைவீணையரியாழினரொருபா
    லிருக்கொடுதோத்திரமியம்பினரொருபாற்
றுன்னியபிணைமலர்க்கையினரொருபாற்
    றொழுகையரழுகையர்துவள்கையரொருபாற்
சென்னியிலஞ்சலிகூப்பினரொருபாற்
    றிருப்பெருந்துறையுறைசிவபெருமானே
யென்னையுமாண்டுகொண்டின்னருள்புரியு
    மெம்பெருமான்பள்ளியெழுந்தருளாயே.

119 உடையாளுன்றனடுவிருக்குமுடையாணடுவுணீ
    யிருத்தி
யடியேனடுவுளிருவீருமிருப்பதானாலடியேனுன்
னடியார்நடுவுளிருக்குமருளைப்புரியாய்பொன்
    னம்பலத்தெம்
முடியாமுதலேயென்கருத்துமுடியும்வண்ண
    முன்னின்றே.

118. On this side some men play
Lutes and vīṇas sweet of sound;
On that side some men chant
Ancient Ṛik, their songs resound;
In their hands some have brought
Wreaths of many blossoms wove;
Some bow down, some men weep,
Some men sway, o'ercome by love;

Clasping hands o'er their heads,
Others stand with reverent air;
Śiva, Lord, dweller in
Holy Perunduṛai fair,
Even me didst thou save;
Sweet to me have been Thy ways.
Now, O Lord of us all,
From Thy couch rise in Thy grace.

---

The rest of our specimens of the 'Holy Utterances' may be left to explain themselves without comment, save for a single line of title. Where two or more stanzas are given from a poem, the title here given is a translation from the Tamil.

### ONLY WITH THEE AND THY SAINTS!

119. Our lady aye is in Thy heart,
As Thou in hers; and if ye both
In mine do dwell, grant me a part
Among your slaves, O ever First.
Unending lord, in Tillai's hall who dost abide,
Let this deep yearning of my soul be satisfied.

120 தந்ததுன்றன்னைக்கொண்டதென்றன்னைச்
சங்கராவார்கொலோசதுர
ரந்தமொன்றில்லாவானந்தம்பெற்றே
னியாதுநீபெற்றதொன்றென்பாற்
சிந்தையேகோயில்கொண்டவெம்பெருமான்
றிருப்பெருந்துறையுறைசிவனே
யெந்தையேயீசாவுடலிடங்கொண்டா
யானிதற்கிலனோர்கைம்மாறே.

121 வெஞ்சேலனையகண்ணார்தம்வெகுளிவலையிலகப்
பட்டு
நைஞ்சேனாயேன்ஞானச்சுடரேநானோர்துணைகா
ணேன்
பஞ்சேரடியாள்பாகத்தொருவாபவளத்திரு
வாயா
லஞ்சேலென்னவாசைப்பட்டேன்கண்டாயம்
மானே.

122 பாரொடுவிண்ணாய்ப்பரந்தவெம்பரனே
பற்றுநான்மற்றிலேன்கண்டாய்
சீரொடுபொலிவாய்சிவபுரத்தரசே
திருப்பெருந்துறையுறைசிவனே
யாரொடுநோகேனார்க்கெடுத்துரைக்கே
னாண்டநீயருளிலையானால்
வார்கடலுலகில்வாழ்கிலேன்கண்டாய்
வருகவென்றருள்புரியாயே.

### What Can I Give Thee?

120. Thou gav'st Thyself, Thou gained'st me;
Which did the better bargain drive?
Bliss found I in infinity;
But what didst Thou from me derive?
O Śiva, Perunduṛai's God,
My mind Thou tookest for Thy shrine:
My very body's Thine abode:
What can I give Thee, Lord, of mine?

---

### Passion's Pain

121. Caught am I in passion's snare from women's liquid eyes;
Stabbed at heart, a cur. O wisdom's light, no aid I see.
Only lord, whose lady's feet are softer than the down,
How I long to hear Thy coral lips speak cheer to me.

### Longings for Death

122. Our lord supreme, both earth and heav'n indwelling,
See how I have no other help but Thee.
Thou king of Śiva's world, bright beyond telling,
Dweller in Perunduṛai, look on me.
Who'll hear my cry, who list to my complaining,
If Thou Thy grace deny, who saved'st me?
I find in sea-girt earth no joy remaining.
Now let Thy grace speak, bid me come to Thee.

123 பஞ்சின்மெல்லடியாள்பங்கநீயல்லாற்
பற்றுநான்மற்றிலேன்கண்டாய்
செஞ்சவேயாண்டாய்சிவபுரத்தரசே
திருப்பெருந்துறையுறைசிவனே
யஞ்சினேனாயேனாண்டுநீயளித்த
வருளினைமருளினான்மறந்த
வஞ்சனேனிங்குவாழ்கிலேன்கண்டாய்
வருகவென்றருள்புரியாயே.

124 பழுதிறொல்புகழாள்பங்கநீயல்லாற்
பற்றுநான் மற்றிலேன்கண்டாய்
செழுமதியணிந்தாய்சிவபுரத்தரசே
திருப்பெருந்துறையுறைசிவனே
தொழுவனோ பிறரைத்துதிப்பனோவெனக்கோர
துணையென நினைவனோ சொல்லாய்
மழவிடையானே வாழ்கிலேன்கண்டாய்
வருகவென்றருள் புரியாயே.

125 பிணக்கிலாதபெருந்துறைப்பெரு
மானுன்னாமங்கள்பேசுவார்க்
கிணக்கிலாததோரின்பமேவருந்
துன்பமேதுடைத்தெம்பிரா
னுணக்கிலாததோர்வித்துமேல்விளை
யாமலென்வினையொத்தபின்
கணக்கிலாத்திருக்கோலநீவந்து
காட்டினாய்கழுக்குன்றிலே.

123. In Thee she dwells whose feet than down are softer;
See how I have no other help but Thee.
Thou king of Śiva's world, my gracious master,
Dweller in Perunduṛai, look on me.
Fear holds me; for, in dark confusion godless,
I did forget the grace that savèd me.
Dog and deceitful am I. Life is joyless.
Now let Thy grace speak, bid me come to Thee.

124. In Thee she dwells whose ancient praise is faultless;
See how I have no other help but Thee.
Thou king of Śiva's world, the bright moon wearing,
Dweller in Perunduṛai, look on me.
Whom save Thee could I worship with my praises?
Can any other refuge give for me?
O Rider of the bull, my life is joyless.
Now let Thy grace speak, bid me come to Thee.

---

### The Balancing of Deeds

125. O lord of Perunduṛai, place of peace,
To them who call Thy name, beyond compare
True joy art Thou. Thou mad'st my woe to cease
When good and ill deeds done were balanced fair.
Then lest unwith'ring seeds of-birth should grow,
In Kaḻukunḍa Thy fair self didst shew.

126 எனைநானென்பதறியேன்பகலிரவாவதுமறியேன்
மனவாசகங்கடந்தானெனைமத்தோன்மத்தனுக்கிச்
சினமால்விடையுடையான்மன்னுதிருப்பெருந்துறையுறையும்
பனவனெனைச்செய்தபடிறறியேன்பரஞ்சுடரே.

127 வேண்டேன்புகழ்வேண்டேன்செல்வம்வேண்டேன்மண்ணும்விண்ணும்
வேண்டேன்பிறப்பிறப்புச்சிவம்வேண்டார்தமைநாளுந்
தீண்டேன்சென்றுசேர்ந்தேன்மன்னு திருப்பெருந்துறையிறைதாள்
பூண்டேன்புறம்போகேனினிப்புறம்போகலொட்டேனே.

128 கோற்றேனெனக்கென்கோகுரைகடல்வாயமுதென்கோ
வாற்றேனெங்களரனேயருமருந்தேயெனதரசே
சேற்றார்வயல்புடைசூழ்தருதிருப்பெருந்துறையுறையு
நீற்றார்தருதிருமேனிநின்மலனேயுனையானே.

129 வான்பாவியவுலகத்தவர்தவமேசெயவவமே
யூன்பாவியவுடலைச்சுமந்தடவிமரமானேன்
றேன்பாய்மலர்க்கொன்றைமன்னுதிருப்பெருந்துறையுறைவாய்
நான்பாவியனானாலுனைநல்காயெனலாமே.

### Life's Consuming

126. Myself I cannot understand, nor what is day nor night;
He who both word and thought transcends has reft my senses quite,
He who for bull has Vishṇu, and in Perunduṛai dwells,
O Light supreme, in Brāhman guise has cast on me strange spells.

127. I ask not fame, wealth, earth or heav'n. No birth, no death for me.
None will I touch who love not Śiva. Now 'tis mine to see
Abiding Perunduṛai, wear the King's foot as my crown;
Never will I leave this His shrine, nor let Him leave His own.

128. Art Thou like honey on the branch too high for me to climb?
Or art Thou nectar ocean-churned? O Hara, King sublime,
In Perunduṛai, circled with moist fields, I can see Thee
With form ash-smeared, the spotless. Can I bear my ecstasy?

129. Many in this great earth who live do penance; I alone
Bearing this frame of flesh, a barren jungle-tree have grown.
Dweller in Perunduṛai old where blooms the kondai tree,
May I the sinner cry "Wilt Thou not grant Thyself to me"?

130 புற்றில்வாளரவுமஞ்சேன்பொய்யர்தம்மெய்யு
மஞ்சேன்
கற்றைவார்சடையெம்மண்ணல்கண்ணுதல்பா
தநண்ணி
மற்றுமோர்தெய்வந்தன்னையுண்டெனநினைந்
தெம்பெம்மாற்
கற்றிலாதவரைக்கண்டாலம்மநாமஞ்சுமாறே.

131 வன்புலால்வேலுமஞ்சேன்வளைக்கையார்கடைக்
கணஞ்சே
னென்பெலாமுருகநோக்கியம்பலத்தாடுகின்ற
வென்பொலாமணியையேத்தியினிதருள்பருக
மாட்டா
வன்பிலாதவரைக்கண்டாலம்மநாமஞ்சுமாறே.

132 உம்பர்கட்கரசேயொழிவறநிறைந்த
யோகமேயூற்றையேன்றனக்கு
வம்பெனப்பழுத்தென்குடிமுழுதாண்டு
வாழ்வறவாழ்வித்தமருந்தே
செம்பொருட்டுணிவேசீருடைக்கழலே
செல்வமேசிவபெருமானே
யெம்பொருட்டுன்னைச்சிக்கெனப்பிடித்தே
னெங்கெழுந்தருளுவதினியே.

### Pious Fear

130. I fear not serpents lurking smooth ;
I fear no liars' feignèd truth ;
But when I see fools venturing
E'en to the foot of Him our king,
Our three-eyed Lord with matted hair,
Of His great godhead unaware,
Fools thinking other gods can be,
Terror such sight inspires in me.

131. I fear no javelin's gory blade ;
Nor sidelong glance of bangled maid ;
But when I see men void of grace
Drinking no sweetness from the praise
Of my unchiselled Gem, whose dance
In Tillai's hall is seen, whose glance
Melts men's whole frame in ecstasy,
Terror such sight inspires in me.

### I Cling to Thee

132. King of the heavenly ones! All-filling Excellence!
E'en to vile me Thou Thy wonders hast shown ;
Balm of true bliss, ending false earthly bliss of sense,
Thou my whole household did'st take for Thine own.
Meaning of holy writ! Wondrous Thy glory!
True wealth, our Śiva, to Thee, Lord, I cling.
Never to loose my hold, firmly I cling to Thee ;
Where canst Thou go, leaving me sorrowing?

133 விடைவிடாதுகந்தவிண்ணவர்கோவே
வினையனேனுடையமெய்ப்பொருளே
முடைவிடாதடியேன்மூத்தறமண்ணாய்
முழுப்புழுக்குரம்பையிற்கிடந்து
கடைபடாவண்ணங்காத்தெனையாண்ட
கடவுளேகருணைமாகடலே
யிடைவிடாதுன்னைச்சிக்கெனப்பிடித்தே
னெங்கெழுந்தருளுவதினியே.

134 புன்புலால்யாக்கைபுரைபுரைகனியப்
பொன்னெடுங்கோயிலாப்புகுந்தென்
னென்பெலாமுருக்கியெளியையாயாண்ட
வீசனேயாசிலாமணியே
துன்பமேபிறப்பேயிறப்பொடுமயக்காந்
தொடக்கெலாமறுத்தநற்சோதீ
யின்பமேயுன்னைச்சிக்கெனப்பிடித்தே
னெங்கெழுந்தருளுவதினியே.

135 உற்றாரையான்வேண்டேனூர்வேண்டேன்பேர்
வேண்டேன்
கற்றாரையான்வேண்டேன்கற்பனவுமினியமை
யுங்
குற்றாலத்தமர்ந்துறையுங்கூத்தாவுன்குரைக
ழற்கே
கற்றாவின்மனம்போலக்கசிந்துருகவேண்டுவனே.

133. King of celestial ones, ever with bull for steed,
Evil am I, yet my riches art Thou;
Lest I should rot in my foul flesh, and die indeed,
Thou hast preserved me, and Thine am I now.
Thou art our God; Thou of grace art a boundless sea,
Saved from my flesh, now to Thee, Lord, I cling.
Never to let Thee loose, firmly I cling to Thee;
Where can'st Thou go, leaving me sorrowing?

134. Thou dids't come into my vile fleshly body,
E'en as 'twere into some great golden shrine;
Soft'ning and melting it all, Thou hast savèd me,
Lord condescending, Thou gem all divine!
Sorrow and birth, death, all ties that deceivèd me,
Thou did'st remove, all my bonds severing;
True bliss, our kindly Light, firmly I cling to Thee;
Where canst Thou go leaving me sorrowing?

### Naught but Thy Love

135. I ask not kin, nor name, nor place,
Nor learnèd men's society.
Men's lore for me no value has;
Kuttālam's lord, I come to Thee.
Wilt thou one boon on me bestow,
A heart to melt in longing sweet,
As yearns o'er new-born calf the cow,
In yearning for Thy sacred feet?

136 சீலமின்றிநோன்பின்றிச்செறிவேயின்றியறிவின்
றித்
தோலின்பாவைக்கூத்தாட்டாய்ச்சுழன்றுவிழுந்
துகிடப்பேனை
மாலுங்காட்டிவழிகாட்டிவாராவுலகநெறியேறக்
கோலங்காட்டியாண்டானைக்கொடியேனென்றோ
கூடுவதே.

137 முத்திநெறியறியாதமூர்க்கரொடுமுயல்வேனைப்
பத்திநெறியறிவித்துப்பழவினைகள்பாறும்வண்
ணஞ்
சித்தமலமறுவித்துச்சிவமாக்கியெனையாண்ட
வத்தனெனக்கருளியவாறார்பெறுவாரச்சோவே.

138 நெறியல்லாநெறிதன்னைநெறியாகநினைவேனைச்
சிறுநெறிகள்சேராமேதிருவருளேசேரும்வண்ணங்
குறியொன்றுமில்லாதகூத்தன்றன்கூத்தையெ
னக்
கறியும்வண்ணமருளியவாறார்பெறுவாரச்சோவே.

### Longing for Union

136. I had no virtue, penance, knowledge, self-control.
A doll to turn
At others' will I danced, whirled, fell. But me
He filled in every limb
With love's mad longing, and that I might climb
there whence is no return,
He shewed His beauty, made me His. Ah me,
when shall I go to Him?

### The Wonder of Grace

137. Fool's friend was I, none such may know
The way of freedom; yet to me
He shew'd the path of love, that so
Fruit of past deeds might ended be.
Cleansing my mind so foul, He made me like
a god.
Ah who could win that which the Father hath
bestowed?

138. Thinking it right, sin's path I trod;
But, so that I such paths might leave,
And find His grace, the dancing God,
Who far beyond our thought doth live,
O wonder passing great!—to me His dancing
shewed.
Ah who could win that which the Father hath
bestowed?

# APPENDIX I

## SHRINES MENTIONED IN THESE POEMS

Āduturai, or Āvaduturai, in Tanjore District, now a station on the South Indian Railway.
Aiyāru, twelve miles from Tanjore.
Ālavāy, or Uttarakosaimangai, Madura.
Aṇṇāmalai, or Tiruvaṇṇāmalai, in South Arcot District.
Ārūr, Tiruvallur, Tanjore District.
Athihai Virattāṇam, South Arcot District.
Bramāpuram, Shiyali, Tanjore District.
Chenkāttankuḍi
Chidambaram, or Tillai, or Perumpattapuliyūr, in S. Arcot District, the most venerated place of Saivism.
Chōḷa, one of the three great kingdoms into which the ancient Tamil country was divided.
Comorin, extreme southern point of India, still a great place of pilgrimage.
Dharmapuram, near Tranquebar, Tanjore District.
Kāviri, or Cauvery, the most sacred river in South India.
Kachchi Ehambam, or Kānchipuram, the modern Conjeeveram, in North Arcot District.
Keḍila
Kētāram
Koḍumuḍi, near Erode, Coimbatore District.
Kōḷili, near the modern Tiruvallur, Tanjore District.
Kongu
Kundaiyūr, near Tiruvallur, Tanjore District.
Kuttālam, Tanjore District.
Maḷapādi, South Arcot District, near Trichinopoly.
Maṛaikkādu, the modern Vetharaniam, Tanjore District. Curiously enough, the modern name is the Sanskrit translation of the Tamil, meaning 'Forest of the Vedas,' *i.e.*, lonely place where Vedas are studied.
Maruhal, on the Cauvery River, Tanjore District.
Neyttānam, on the Cauvery River, Tanjore District.
Ottiyūr, better known as Tiruvottiyur, a few miles north of Madras, now practically a suburb.
Paḷanam, Tanjore District.
Perumpattapuliyur, see Chidambaram.
Perunduṛai, Āvudaiyārkoil, Tanjore District.
Puhalūr
Pungūr, seven miles from Shiyāli, Tanjore District.
Pūnturutti
Puvaṇam, twelve miles from Madura.
Tillai, see Chidambaram.
Tiruputtūr, Ramnad District, near Pudukottah.
Tiruvaṇṇāmalai, see Aṇṇāmalai.
Tiru Neyttānam, see Neyttānam.
Tūngānaimādam
Uttarakōsamangai, Ramnad District.
Valivalam, on the Cauvery, Tanjore District.
Venneynallūr, South Arcot District.

*N.B.*—"Tiru" is an epithet meaning "Holy," but where it has become practically part of the place-name, that name is given in this list as if it began with T.

# APPENDIX II

## SYSTEM OF TRANSLITERATION AND PRONUNCIATION OF TAMIL LETTERS

| Tamil | Sanskrit | English | Pronunciation (approximate) |
|---|---|---|---|
| அ | अ | a | u in punch |
| ஆ | आ | ā | ā in rather |
| இ | इ | i | i in sit |
| ஈ | ई | ī | ī in clique |
| உ | उ | u | u in full |
| ஊ | ऊ | ū | ū in rule |
| எ | — | e | e in fed |
| ஏ | ए | ē | a in fable |
| ஐ | ऐ | ai | ai in aisle, but much shorter |
| ஒ | — | o | o in mobility |
| ஓ | ओ | ō | ō in noble |
| ஔ | औ | au | ow in cow |

### CONSONANTS

*N.B.*—The Tamil alphabet is not fully phonetic as are the Sanskrit and the other Dravidian alphabets. Several letters indicate different sounds in different connections.

| Letter | 1. When mute 2. In the beginning of a word 3. After a hard consonant | After a soft consonant | In other places | Remarks |
|---|---|---|---|---|
| க் | k (क्) | g (ग्) | h (ह्) | Guttural. |
| ச் | ch (च्) | j (ज्) | s (स्) | This is pronounced as a *palatal* sibilant. |
| ட் | ṭ (ट्) | ḍ (ड्) | ḍ | Cerebral, far back in the palate. |
| த் | t (त्) | d (द्) | th | Dental purer than English dentals. |
| ப் | p (प्) | b (ब्) | p | Labial. |
| ற் | *t* | *d* | *r* | Hard palatal ṛ, peculiar to Tamil as pronounced after a soft consonant. |

| Tamil | Sanskrit | Transliteration | Pronunciation (approximate) | Remarks |
|---|---|---|---|---|
| ங் | ङ् | ṅ (before g) | n in singing | guttural n |
| ஞ் | ञ् | ñ | n in ginger | palatal n |
| ண் | ण् | ṇ | n stopped as far back as possible | cerebral n |
| ந் & ன் | न् | n | as in English | |
| ம் | म् | m | as in English | |
| ய் | य् | y | as in English | |
| ர் | र् | r | as in English (when soft) | |
| ல் | ल् | l | as in English | |
| வ் | व् | v | as in English, but not so firm | |
| ழ் | — | ḻ | r pronounced with the tongue as far back in the throat as possible. | Peculiar to Tamil |
| ள் | ळ् | ḷ | l pronounced by the palate | palatal l |

Sanskrit words, unless they have become modified by long Tamil usage, as, for example, in the author's name Māṇikka Vāsahar, are transliterated according to Sanskrit pronunciation, on the system used in other books in this series, the Sanskrit alphabet being represented as follows :—

| | | | | |
|---|---|---|---|---|
| k | kh | g | gh | ṅ |
| ch | chh | j | jh | ñ |
| ṭ | ṭh | ḍ | ḍh | ṇ |
| t | th | d | dh | n |
| p | ph | b | bh | m |
| y | r | l | v | |
| ś | sh | s | h | |
| ṛi | ṁ | ḥ | | |

# INDEX

(THE NUMBERS ARE THOSE OF PAGES, NOT OF STANZAS.)